Ski THE CANADIAN WAY

David Ritchie

and Members of the Canadian National Ski Team

Prentice-Hall of Canada, Ltd.
Scarborough, Ontario

For

Ken and Jane Ritchie
Bill and Dill Murray
Bill and Mary Irwin
John and Dee Read
Michael and Jacqueline Podborski

Canadian Cataloguing in Publication Data

Ritchie, David, 1952-
Ski the Canadian way

ISBN 0-13-809780-1

1. Ski racing. I. Canadian National Ski Team.
II. Title.

GV854.9.R3R58 796.9'3 C79-094728-5

Prentice-Hall, Inc., Englewood Cliffs, New Jersey
Prentice-Hall International, Inc., London
Prentice-Hall of Australia, Pty., Ltd., Sydney
Prentice-Hall of India, Pvt., Ltd., New Delhi
Prentice-Hall of Japan, Inc., Tokyo
Prentice-Hall of Southeast Asia (Pte.) Ltd., Singapore

ISBN 0-13-809780-1

Production Editors: Jan Whitford/Barbara Steel
Design and Illustrations: Julian Cleva

Every reasonable effort has been made to contact holders of photograph copyrights. The publishers would be pleased to have any errors or omissions brought to their attention.

Photos, pp vi, viii, x by permission of Salomon North America.

front cover photograph: *David Murray in Shell Cup downhill at Lake Louise*
photograph by Harvey Soicher

Printed and bound in Canada

1 2 3 4 5 AP 83 82 81 80 79

Contents

14

Acknowledgements

The authors are grateful for the kind assistance of Shell Canada Ltd., Molson Breweries of Canada Ltd., and Salomon Bindings, Ltd., and wish to express their thanks to the Canadian Ski Association, FIS, Ski Canada magazine and Terry Spence for his enlightening insights.

Foreword

The Canadian Ski Association is proud of the results achieved by its skiers over the years and the current downhill team, by its performances in the 1978/79 season, is strengthening the status of Canada at the international level.

These results do not just happen; they are the culmination of long hours of planning, conditioning and training and represent the input of many volunteers and professional staff whose support is necessary along with the dedication of the athletes themselves.

The aims and objectives of the Association can be simply stated. They are:

1) To enable participants to achieve their personal potential in the sport of skiing.
2) To encourage increased competitive participation.
3) To enhance the personal human growth and development of the individual competitors.

When one competes, one competes to win. Our downhill team is a wonderful example of this philosophy.

John Newton
Executive Director,
CSA

Introduction

Downhill skiing is the most glamorous and exciting of all the alpine disciplines. An elite group of its competitors, all with a number of World Cup medals to their credit and considerable international fame, have collaborated to write this book, revealing the secrets of their success.

Courage, technique, and ambition to win are not the sole properties of any one nation or any one skier. However, over the course of racing's history, several nations have had their turn at domination. The sixties were called the French era in international skiing. In the seventies, the Austrians, Swiss and Italians each had a turn. In the late seventies, the Canadians held top spot in the men's World Cup downhill, while their American counterparts excelled in slalom and giant slalom.

The all-out attack with which the Canadians approached the downhill earned them nicknames like "The Kamikaze Kids" or "Crazy Canucks" from the European press. But while this method has proved extremely successful, there is more to winning a World Cup downhill than careening wildly down a mountain. A win comes as the result of long hard hours of training the body specifically for the sport, developing the best technique, testing the most sophisticated equipment. This book tells how many of the factors that made the Canadians into champions can be used by both recreational and more aggressive skiers to improve their performance on the slopes.

Because racing represents the fastest way to ski, the competitor must develop the most efficient technique. As Nancy Greene, the first woman to be awarded the World Cup, has said, "Strange as it may seem, the high demands of competition usually develop the simplest technique. The quick reactions needed for the competitive turn allow no time for fancy frills and inefficient body movements. It should be easy to see that there are lessons the beginner can learn from ski racing. . . . the simplest method is best for everyone." (*Alpine Skiing,* p. 11)

This book will be useful for recreational skiers and young racers as well as spectators. It will teach skiers how to improve performance and reach their goal faster and more easily, no matter how basic or ambitious it may be. It will acquaint spectators with the excitement of World Cup and Olympic ski competition, and take them on a tour of seven of the greatest downhill sites in the world. It will teach young racers how to cope with such problems as the threat of injury and conquering fear, choosing the fastest line down the mountainside, and improving overall performance.

The authors of this book are not professional sports writers but the skiers themselves. They have passed through all the stages in learning a challenging and exhilarating sport, and have emerged on the top. Winners. Gods of the mountain.

10

CHAPTER ONE

The White Circus

A travelling entertainment featuring feats of skill, daring and pageantry: what more appropriate title could the French have found for the World Cup Circuit than the White Circus, "La Cirque Blanche"?

This particular circus takes places on the snow-covered peaks of some thirteen countries. The slopes are sometimes familiar, but often virtually unknown to the 80 or 85 racers representing at least sixteen different nations. The circuit is designed to include races in all three disciplines — slalom, giant slalom and downhill. In the 1978-79 season, thirty-three races were scheduled, ten of which were World Cup downhills. In the 1979-80 season seven of the twenty-three races scheduled were downhills.

The circus procession commences in December and rambles for four months from Europe to Japan, the USA and Scandinavia. This is an exciting time for the alpine populace, whose numbers grow by the thousands for World Cup week. Aside from the Olympic Games, the World Cup is the most prestigious event in organized amateur skiing.

History of the World Cup

The first World Cup event was staged in 1967 when the vision of a European sports journalist, Serge Lang, became a reality. Prior to that year, race results were a rather haphazard compilation of who won which race where. Racers had to wait for the Olympics for a true World Champion to be decided. Lang, himself a skier, conceived an international competition modelled on international auto racing. In Grand Prix auto racing, a yearly championship is decided by the drivers' overall results in a pre-selected number of rallies during the entire racing season. Lang suggested that a number of races in all three alpine disciplines be chosen from the annual FIS calendar, and that these count towards World Cup points. Once this World Cup had been established, annual international champions could be recognized.

In 1967, Jean-Claude Killy of France and Nancy (Tiger) Greene of Canada became the first World Cup champions. In later years such world-renowned figures as Karl Schranz, Gustavo Thoeni, Ingemar Stenmark, Anne-Marie Moser-Proëll and Rosie Mittermaier were named World Cup champions.

The Rules

Selected World Cup races, held between December 1st and March 31st of each year, are used to determine World Cup champions for alpine skiing. As of the 1978-79 season World Cup points are awarded to the top 15 finishers in a race, as follows:

by permission of Salomon

Sign posts indicate the way to Villars, France, host of a World Cup downhill in 1978. Ski teams often travel long hours by car in all winter conditions throughout Europe.

Franz Maier

European fans gather to watch the excitement of World Cup competition.

Rank	World Cup Points
1	25
2	20
3	15
4	12
5	11
6	10
7	9
8	8
9	7
10	6
11	5
12	4
13	3
14	2
15	1

Each season, the number of competitions is subject to change. In 1979-80, seven downhill events, eight slalom events, eight giant slalom events and four combined events are scheduled.

Each year individual World Cups are awarded by the FIS in each of the first three disciplines, to the skier who accumulates the highest point total in his five best results in that discipline. In 1979-80 there will also be four combined events, two of downhill and slalom and two of downhill and giant slalom. To receive high points in the combined, a skier must do well in both disciplines. For example, if he were to win both the downhill and the slalom, he would receive 25 points for the downhill win, 25 points for the slalom win and 25 points for the combined win. The Combined World Cup is then presented to the skier who has accumulated the most points in his best three of the four combined events.

In the event of a tie in any of the four individual disciplines, the racer with the most victories or the best placings would take the championship. In the event of any ties among the top 6 finishers in overall World Cup competition the competitor's total points earned would be taken, not just points from his two best combined events or five best finishes in the other three. Further ties would be broken by taking into consideration the number of placings in individual events of the competitor.

In the past, skiers were expected to participate in all events, including the nordic ones. Today this is inconceivable. Since the start of the World Cup in 1967, each discipline has become highly specialized. To be consistently successful in any one of them takes all a racer's concentration and a great deal of specialized training.

Nevertheless, FIS also awards two overall World Cup championships to the man and woman who have accumulated the highest number of total points from all four disciplines. The four best results are taken from downhill, giant slalom and slalom, and the two best results are taken from the combined event.

by permission of F.M.H.

David Irwin makes a high speed turn in Schladming, December 1979. The lack of snow forced organizers to truck it in to cover the course.

In 1978, World Cup scoring changes set the maximum number of points which each skier could count from any one of the 4 categories — downhill, slalom, giant slalom and combined — at 75. This made it virtually impossible for the specialist to win the overall World Cup.

In the 1978-79 season, for instance, Peter Luescher of Switzerland defeated Sweden's Ingemar Stenmark for the overall World Cup title, although he had only defeated Stenmark in one slalom event, whereas Stenmark won an unprecedented 13 consecutive races. However, since he specialized only in giant slalom and slalom he was allowed to collect a maximum of 150 points. Peter Luescher's participation in downhill as well resulted in his earning points both in that discipline and in the combined and defeating Stenmark for the overall title. Stenmark, winner of many World Cup overall titles in past years, now had to be satisfied with only individual titles. However, because of the uproar which this situation caused, changes have been made in the rules which allow a slalom and giant slalom specialist to win the overall title without competing in the downhill, as long as he has dominated the other two events throughout the season.

Life on the World Cup Trail

The World Cup Downhill is one of Europe's flashiest and most exciting sporting events. It is followed by millions of enthusiastic fans on European television and live spectators number in the tens of thousands. For a European ski resort to earn the right to host a World Cup competition is a great honor and brings with it a terrific promotional advantage.

There is big money in European ski races. Resorts lobby for years at great expense to be scheduled on the World Cup Calendar. The lack of snow in Schladming, Austria during the 1978-79 season did not deter the race organizers from hosting the World Cup event in this tiny alpine village. The course was worked on for 4 days by 220 men and 27 dump trucks, hauling snow to the mountains. Schladming, a candidate for the 1982 World Championships, wanted to show the world that it could put on a race under any conditions. It did a fantastic job. For the traditional race sites such as Kitzbühel, Austria, the World Cup media coverage constitutes the year's promotion for the community.

The ski racer is worshipped as a hero by the fans who follow the races from site to site around Europe. The crowds in lift line-ups stand aside to let team members in training cut in front. Even the European governments are much more serious about ski racing: they are well aware of its importance to tourism and national prestige.

Until very recently, skiing was not a big spectator sport in Canada or the USA. It used to be that when a World Cup race booked into an area like Whistler or Lake Louise it did not draw spectators, it only disrupted normal operations. With their winter fixation on hockey, most Canadians don't realize yet how big and exciting downhill racing is — and how strong Canada has become in the sport. But North American ski areas are beginning to realize the benefits available to them from the extensive media coverage and they, too, are starting to compete to host races.

The downhill boasts a certain mystique among the general public, even in North America. The other two technical events — slalom and giant slalom — are somewhat boring in comparison. ABC, for instance, televises two downhills a year, but has yet to broadcast its first slalom, an event which American Phil Mahre is perfectly capable of winning.

Prior to the arrival of the World Cup entourage, weeks of preparations are made by a highly trained task force of experienced race organizers at the site. By the time the Canadian team rolls into town, the excitement of World Cup fever has already struck. The race office is full of masses of tourists struggling to find their hotels and get accreditation passes and race information.

by permission of Ski Canada Magazine

Canadians find a piece of home at a familiar restaurant in France.

Ski villages are filled with banners, cheering children and milling crowds conversing in many languages about the White Circus. The press corps, 350 radio and television reporters, photographers and technicians, is busy hooking up telex machines, securing extra phone lines or finding photoprocessing labs.

Technicians unload the confusion of miles of cables and discs from their tractor trailers. Cameras are lowered from helicopters onto strategic mounts positioned along the downhill course.

Team Organization

By European standards, the Canadian National Team is small, with unorthodox methods. It certainly is a long way from the sophistication of the larger European teams of Austria and Switzerland. These teams have their entire country's tourist and ski manufacturing industries behind them. They can afford luxuries like delivery of skis to the starting line by helicopter. When the Austrian team moves, it's like an army breaking camp.

Because the Canadian and American teams are so far from home, they are at something of a disadvantage. They can afford neither the time nor the money for trips to home bases in Canada and the US. They can spend up to four or five months on the road, and every hotel along the way has to serve as home for a few days. The team is organized as much as possible to minimize the effects of travel and cultural differences. Plans are made well in advance for transporting and storing equipment and housing the skiers: there are no worries about where they will be staying or whether or not the exchange rate is right.

Of course, one of the biggest problems of travelling in Europe is language, and being a bilingual (French and English) Canadian is not a great help. Eighty percent of the time on the circuit is spent in German-speaking countries, and most team members can now get by well enough in that language to talk to ski officials, other racers and the European media. Assistant coach, Heinz Kappler, a European fluent in 5 languages, helps immensely in coping with the communication problems.

Regardless of all the planning and organization which goes into travel, it is still physically exhausting. When Ken Read of Calgary arrived in Mount Tremblant, Quebec, to compete in the Canadian Alpine Ski Championships for the Shell Cup at the end of the 1978-79 World Cup season he complained "I'm almost saying to myself, 'What am I doing here? It's a beautiful, sunny day, 80 degrees, but my body is somewhere over the Pacific Ocean. I am physically exhausted. The only place I want to be is in bed'." Read was in the starting gate ready to race less than 24 hours after a 17-hour flight from Furano, Japan where he had competed in a giant slalom event just a few days earlier.

Jet lag and fatigue are all part of the sport. A racer has to get used to it or at least learn to live with it. He is helped in this by the disciplined routine he follows daily. Despite the glamor and excitement of traveling in Europe, the life of a World Cup skier is very regimented. Every day there is a schedule to be followed. There is little time for being a tourist or enjoying the night life at exotic restaurants. After arriving at an area skiers have 3 days of training before each World Cup downhill race. Each racer must have 3 timed training runs before he can officially enter the race.

A typical training day goes something like this. Wakeup is at 7:00, whether skiers are racing or not. A few minutes are spent doing stretching exercises and calisthenics, after which skiers don training suits and go for a 15-minute run through the narrow European streets, just as the town begins to wake for the day. At 8:00 a.m. they breakfast on the typical European fare of coffee and sweet rolls. (Ken Read is reputed to have the best dry cereal mix on the circuit: nuts, seeds, bran, muesli and oats, usually topped with sliced bananas.) At 8:30 it's time to prepare for training on the course. Once dressed, team members go to the ski room to pick up poles and three pairs of skis. One pair is for free skiing and an inspection run on the course. The other two pairs are used for the two scheduled training runs. Generally, skiers are at the start by 9:30. This gives them about an hour and a half before training begins. Most of this time is spent warming up by free skiing. It's always best to start out slowly, turning back and forth to regain the feel of skiing. The second free-skiing run is a little faster and the speed increases with subsequent runs until the skiers are highly confident.

Just prior to the first training run of the day the Canadians warm up in the lodge, leaving skis outside on the snow to cool the bases to snow temperature. Coaches John Ritchie and Heinz Kappler discuss the condition of the snow and the course in general. Then it's on to the top of that mountain.

The world's skiing elite gather round the starting gate awaiting the okay for the first inspection down the new course. A friendly but concentrated atmosphere surrounds the competitors as they make their way down the hill, and there is much good-willed advice requested and given among the racers. Everyone is apprehensive about that first high speed run coming up. That common adversary unifies the group of sixty to seventy highly competitive individuals, each one aware that the knowledge gained at this time is crucial to a fast and safe week of downhill racing.

Experience is probably the foremost aid in deciphering the riddle presented by a new downhill. Inspection runs are conducted at very slow speeds with frequent stops for careful study of snow conditions and line. Skiers and coaches must attempt to judge the varying speeds involved through each section, and envision the effects of the turns and bumps at these speeds. After a few minutes to warm up in the lodge and discuss any final strategy with the coaches, competitors proceed to the top of the mountain to the start at 11:00 for the first timed training run of the day.

by permission of Salomon

Bindings are checked before every training run and race to help in the prevention of mishaps.

courtesy of Gameplan Information Office

Coaches are stationed at crucial sections of the course and information regarding line and course conditions is communicated to racers at the start.

A Training Run

At the top of the mountain competitors are assembled. Now there is more tension in the air, but the Austrians are eating chocolate bars, wieners and bread. David Murray comments: "There they are — the world's best downhill team before the race, eating Mars bars, wienies and wonderloaf. How do they do it?!" Laughter.

The army of manufacturers' technicians give the final check to the equipment. Coaches and video technicians are spread out all along the course to communicate vital information about the performance of other skiers via two-way radio to their own teams, and then to observe the performance of their own skiers at key points along the course.

Werner Grissmann, once a chimney sweep and now the idol of thousands of young Austrian girls, is first on the course. He starts with a monstrous lunge and a groan befitting his nickname, "the Griss".

The start is alive with two-way radio conversation in six languages as progress reports come in on the racers from all along the course. Heinz Kappler, one of the Canadian coaches, radios, "He's coming into a big bump really fast. People are having trouble there so be ready for it. Stay forward and have a good start!".

The Canadians have set a style of all-out assault during training runs. These are just as dangerous as the actual race and mishaps do occur. But other racers quickly adopted this "Kamikaze" approach to training runs and now every one is an all-out assault on the mountain.

The snow is hard and slick. The course has some big bumps with long air time, but they don't pose too much of a problem. Some of the skiers are having problems in the top turns which they will have to iron out in the next three days before the race. At 12:00 or 1:00 the second timed training run is started. After this second run is over skiers return to their home away from home to join coaches and fellow team members for lunch. The

Lindley photo

American downhiller Andy Mill and Canadian David Irwin discuss results following a compulsory training run. The two national teams often train together in Europe.

trek back to the hotel is often interrupted by autograph seekers and members of the press.

"How did you like the course?" "Who do you think will win?" "What happened to you last week?" At times it seems as if the World Cup Tour is 2 parts skiing, 1 part traveling and 3 parts dealing with the press. At lunch the coach states: "Well boys, you all look good by me. I don't know where you lost your time today but the video was on the top turns. Let's study it tonight. See you at dinner. After the coaches' meeting is over, I'll give you tomorrow's schedule. And boys, don't forget your jogging!"

The constant demands of the press, the fans and training make free time precious. After lunch the skiers have a few hours to relax or to consider how the day or the winter has gone. From 3 o'clock to 6 o'clock they spend their time resting, jogging, getting a full massage from the team's masseur, or washing their laundry in the bathtub! At 7 o'clock the team enjoys dinner: it is policy not to discuss business or skiing at dinner. Following the meal, the team reassembles for the daily meeting and video session. A video tape of each training run is shot and reviewed every day to show the racers how they are performing in technical sections of the course, and how they measure up against all the other top skiers in the competition. The meeting ends about 9:30 and by 10:30 skiers are in bed asleep.

Through all the rigors of travel, the pressures from fans and the press, and the constant high tension and competitive atmosphere, it is sometimes very difficult to stay cheerful and good-natured. Poor morale can definitely affect

by permission of F.M.H.

CP photo

A great skier must not let adverse conditions affect his performance. Ken Read of Canada placed first in this event at Chamonix, France.

courtesy of Gameplan Information Office

Trying to get the edge over the competition: video technicians film racers' runs, coaches relay messages to the racers and assistants record section times.

performance and hence results, and the factors affecting it are often completely out of the skier's control. Winter in the mountains is often severe: white-outs, blizzards, numbing cold. Winds at the top of a course can blow in gusts of up to 65 km/h (40 mph). All the press and media attention is distracting and tiring. Unforeseen problems arise: equipment disappears, team members wear the wrong numbers. And imagine the dismay of the Canadians after the World Cup race at Morzine, France in January, 1979. Steve Podborski drew number 1 and made a fantastic run — 5 seconds faster than his fastest training time of the previous day. All the best downhillers in the world took a run at him and couldn't get within a second of his time until teammate Ken Read, running fourteenth, came down the course. Ken beat Steve's time by 40/100 of a second in one of the greatest races of his career. The Canadian team was elated! They knew they had a victory.

And then disaster. Ken Read and Dave Murray were wearing new racing suits, given to the Canadian team just prior to the race and guaranteed by the manufacturer to be the same material as the suits being worn by the Swiss team. A protest lodged by the Italians after the race led to an investigation: the suits did not meet FIS permeability requirements. Ken Read was disqualified and Steve Podborski emerged the victor.

◁ *Ken Read and Steve Podborski of Canada show elation at their 1-2 victory in Morzine, January 1979, despite Read's eventual disqualification in the event.*

The lifestyle on the World Cup circuit has spawned a team spirit which is all the more remarkable because skiing is essentially an individual sport. Team members spend almost nine months of every year eating, sleeping and training together and each one cares deeply about how the other is doing. Although elated by his success, Podborski considered his victory at Morzine a hollow one: Ken had been ripped off!

But a beautiful sunny morning, with brilliant skies and 8 to 12 inches of fresh powder are enough to lift anyone's spirits.

"If I have to be the fastest guy in the world to be happy, then something is wrong," believes Dave Murray. "Sometimes downhill racing can be so brutal, but yesterday as I was side-slipping down the course I looked up in the sunshine and saw the course with all the gates and realized that this was all for us — for me. And it's fantastic to think that this is our own little playground!"

by permission of Molson Breweries of Canada Ltd.

Fans urge David Murray on at Whistler, B.C., where the 1979 World Cup downhill was cancelled due to technical difficulties.

Race Day at the White Circus

Murray, Podborski, Irwin and Read wake up early that morning, their feet tapping nervously, while their minds flash over the race course one more time, reinforcing the memory of subtle changes in line. Breakfast is light and talkative. They discuss next week, last week, summer plans, everything but the race to be skied that day, straining to catch a glimpse of the course through the steamy, scratched windows. The next time they will see it is during the race run later that day. Noticing the Austrian and German racers among the other skiers, they try to pick up what they are saying and perhaps see what number skis they are bringing up for the race.

The solidarity of the mountain contrasts sharply with the people gathering below. Fans parade up the mountain's face in search of the best point from which to view the race. They will number 40 000 by race time. Some fans carry the results of the week's training runs: helpful information when placing friendly wagers on the day's competition. Some hold tickets to the Swiss Organized Official Lottery called Ski Toto. Some merely share Schnapps and the excitement of the day with their friends. Along the course are banners proclaiming "Go Klammer Go", or "Mueller and Company" and today a Canadian supporter waves the red and white flag to cheer on the Canadian daredevils.

At the start, preparations are being made at a frantic pace. The racers are being pampered by a sophisticated army of ski technicians looking for any slight advantage to give their racers. Valuable last-minute information is being passed on by coaches and course officials, which may mean updating and revising decisions about line. In the confines of the fenced-off area, at the top of the mountain, competitors finally move in single file towards the starting hut. Dave Irwin slips off his warming gear and feels the chill of air through the thin streamlined cut of his yellow racing suit. The constant buzz of the two-way radios with last-minute course reports follows him to the start. Toulouse, his masseur, works to relax the muscles in his thighs, which he refers to as "the jumbos".

He moves to the start and waits anxiously for the last three "beeps", countdown to the start of

Crowds gather at the finish line: Garmisch World Championships, 1978.

by permission of Salomon

the race. He bursts from the start and everything is shut out of his mind except the sensations of wind and snow. In just under two minutes, he has traveled more than two kilometres down the mountain and is flying over the rise leading to the home stretch — the final kilometre. The vibrations of thousands of cheering people and the clanging of alpine cow bells almost knocks him off his skis. There are people lining the course ten deep, all caught up in the World Cup fever as skiers race past the finish to glory.

There is a spray of snow as he skids to a stop after crossing the finish line. The fans cheer. Press microphones surround him. Cameras are directed towards him and a barrage of questions hits him before he can even catch his breath.

There seems to be a madness flowing through the crowd. Autograph seekers mill about in search of their favorite skiing hero. In Europe, autographs of ski racers are traded among children just like hockey cards in Canada or baseball cards in the US.

On one occasion, Dave Irwin was mobbed by youngsters seeking his autograph as he stepped off a bus. "They pinned me against the

Franz Maier

David Murray signs an autograph for one of the "jet setters" at a World Cup race in Kitzbühel, Austria.

by permission of Shell Canada Ltd.

Austria's Peter Wirnsberger discusses his win after the pre-Olympic World Cup race in Lake Placid, 1979.

bus and finally the driver had to clear people away so he could move on."

Another time, Irwin and a few other skiers were stopped in the middle of the street to sign autographs. "After about ten minutes, a policeman made us move along. When I looked up, there were about 50 cars lined up in either direction."

Today, a man grabs Klammer from over the fence. "Hurry! Take the picture!" he yells at his wife. Dozens of children, officially dismissed from school for the day, stretch over the fence and plead for autographs.

Some racers are elated by their success. Others, disappointed at their performance, try to decide where they made their mistakes.

David Irwin begins to make his way through the crowd. Enough of this circus madness! He heads down the hill to avoid the people, and finds himself looking into the sad brown eyes of a little girl, silently beckoning with an outstretched paper and pen. He stops. It was a mistake — the outstretched arms crowd in again. The police finally appear to hold back the fence and the flow of people flooding towards him. He nods his head in acknowledgement and is off again, none too soon. One of the police officers politely appeals, "Bitte, ein Autograph?".

The race is over. For the spectators it's time to return home and capture the day's excitement one more time over the television. With their friends they will discuss questions like "That new Swiss lad who skied fast today, will he win next time? Why is Klammer having problems? The Canadians, will they stay on top?"

After the race the team has the evening to relax, but the next day is a travel day and they rise early, so that most of the driving can be done in daylight. Often, the drive between race sites takes a whole day. Upon arrival the same routine begins again, with one day of free skiing before the training for the next downhill race begins.

Why do they do it? They do it because they love skiing and the challenge of competition. As Coach John Ritchie says, "We would really like to blow the doors off them out there and show the world what Canada is all about".

Franz Maier

Skiing superstar Franz Klammer is followed by autograph-seeking children, officially dismissed from school during World Cup week.

CARRERA

CHAPTER TWO

Techniques

Sound basic technique is the key to success for any skier, especially a racer. A strong foundation in ski technique is needed to perform in any one of the three alpine disciplines, and most downhill specialists are highly accomplished in both slalom and giant slalom. At the level of World Cup competition, technique has become second nature. But as with tournament golfers at the Master's, it is continually being honed in the attempt to reach perfection.

At this level of skiing, most improvements in technique are made for the sake of speed. Skiing through the finish of a World Cup downhill race at Chamonix, France, David Murray found himself in second place behind teammate Ken Read by 16/100 of a second — less than a ski length in distance — after racing the three-kilometer course at an average speed of over 100 km/h. It was his best result in World Cup competition to that point, but like every other racer, he felt first would have been nice!

What is a tenth, or a hundredth of a second? For most people these small measurements of time are meaningless. It is difficult for a layman to understand victories measured in fractions of a second. For the athletes, their actual placing is most indicative of performance, and the time difference between them and their closest competition is of no real consequence, at least for that day and the race just finished. In the long run, though, these fractions are the true measure of the competitors' achievements over the years that they have been racing. The downhill racer lives and breathes the sport of skiing, training and competing for twelve months a year. Working at eliminating seconds becomes an all-encompassing endeavor.

Hard as it may be to believe, the high demands of competition are often best served by the simplest of techniques. There is simply no time for frills or inefficient body movements. The average speed of a downhiller in competition is over 100 km/h. The three-kilometre (two-mile) course is often covered in less than two minutes, and very often race results show fifteen or more competitors finishing within the same second.

Perhaps David Murray has described the relationship between a ski racer and the mountain best: "If the ski racer is a poet of the slopes, the downhill course is his poem with flowing rhythm and defined sections rhyming together to form a three-kilometre track from mountain top to bottom."

The first task for the competitor is to memorize the course. Every change in terrain or direction over the undulating slope must be carefully studied and imprinted on the skier's mind during the hour or so before initial training runs begin. Downhills are broken into sections by coaches and racers. This makes it easier for the skiers to memorize details of the terrain and for the coaches to analyse performance and determine where valuable seconds are being won and lost.

Albrecht Stussi

The start sets the tempo for the entire race. Racers move as far out of the gate as possible before opening the timing wand with their lower body.

by permission of F.M.H.

Steve Podborski shows good speed: this feeling of speed over the snow is one of the true joys of downhill

by permission of F.M.H.

David Murray of Canada maintains his low tuck position while airborne, as he turns through a transition at Schladming, 1978.

by permission of Salomon

Ken Read captures 1st place in world Cup downhill at Chamonix, France.

Leo Mason

A skier moves his upper body down the hill and snaps his lower body from behind. He then takes 2 or 3 strong skates, while pushing hard with his poles.

2-4: Lindley photo

Ken Read assumes a near perfect tuck position across the flats on Lake Placid's Whiteface Mountain.

The Start

There is no better place to begin a description of downhill technique than where the racer first encounters the course. This is no place for the faint of heart. Ahead lies an entire mountain, but the race can be won or lost a fraction of a second after the final starting beep.

The start must be precise. The racer must anticipate the final beep, in order to explode out of the starting gate as fast as possible. The aggressiveness with which the racer leaves the gate sets the mood and flow for the entire run. He must take control of the course immediately, before it takes control of him. In an Olympic downhill event, four years of training and experience will have preceded the competition, and the eventual blast from the gate symbolizes in itself the end of a long struggle and the beginning of a new period in a racer's life.

Most of the power in a good start comes from the arms. The skier pushes back on his poles, while leaping up and out in the same movement. He wants to get as far as possible out of the starting gate with the upper part of the body, before the lower part, maybe even his boots, finally opens the timing wand, located at knee height, and starts the clocks moving.

The first ten meters of hill are usually quite steep. The fastest way for the skier to get moving is to move the upper body down the hill and snap the lower body from behind, then take two or three strong skates, pushing hard with the poles. The amount of skating and poling a skier does will depend on the steepness of the terrain, but even on the flattest of starts, rarely are more than three good pushes needed. Once the maximum speed has been reached, too much skating and poling can actually slow the racer down, because he begins working against himself.

The basic mechanics of a good start must be combined with deep nervous control and heavy concentration. This is no place for a blind attack: the racer must be in complete and aggressive control, physically and mentally.

Unlike motor racing, where a push on the accelerator can compensate for speed lost, downhillers are dependent solely on the force of gravity to carry them at top speed down the course. The initial momentum gained from the start and the first steep pitch must be gathered with care and nursed through one section of the course to the next. This feeling of the mass of one's body carrying speed over the snow must be one of the true joys of downhill racing.

by permission of F.M.H.

The tuck position allows the skier to achieve maximum speed. Although there are several variations in the basic position, it is essential that the skier keep his elbows in and his hands up and together as Steve Podborski demonstrates in his descent at Val Gardena, Italy, 1978.

by permission of F.M.H.

When large arm movements are necessary for balance or driving through a turn, the racer should always keep his hands within the periphery of his vision as Ken Read demonstrates in this wide, high-speed turn.

The Tuck

The tuck is an aerodynamic position used in downhill racing to reduce wind resistance and increase speed. The importance of remaining in a tuck as much as humanly possible during a race cannot be overemphasized. If a skier moves from a tuck position into an upright position, wind resistance will reduce his velocity by as much as one third.

The development of an optimal tuck position and the "feel" of aerodynamics can be learned both on the hill when training and off the hill in a wind tunnel. In the wind tunnel, several different body positions can be tried, and measuring equipment will give the racer instant feedback about the relative speed of each. The optimal position, once found, is then modified in actual on-snow training, to find the most aerodynamic position while on skis. The downhill suit, the restriction of the boots, body manoeuvreability and terrain of the piste must all be taken into consideration in the final choice. The racer is constantly being thrown out of position by the contours of the hill. To the untrained eye, a fast downhill run may appear to be a series of linked recoveries leading toward the finish!

It is only after considerable training and practice that the downhiller develops a "feel" of aerodynamics. This "feel" is an extremely important concept in racing, and one that is learned through kilometer after kilometer and year after year of downhill training. The racer learns to snap into the downhill tuck whenever appropriate.

Although its prime use is during a downhill race, the tuck position can be very helpful to a

by permission of F.M.H.

David Irwin's inner arm is held far back to give his body the necessary rotation to complete the turn. His great strength allowed him to complete the turn successfully without over-rotation, which could have caused loss of control.

recreational skier just prior to a long flat section of the slope. Nature's most natural aerodynamic shape is the egg. To achieve the egg-shaped tuck, a skier can begin practice at home. First, sit down on a chair and bring the upper body down so that the trunk is parallel with the floor. The chest should lie flat on the thighs. Next, stretch the arms out in front of the shins and raise the hands until you are looking directly over them, to see where you are going. Uncomfortable? Hard on the neck? Now have a friend remove the chair. Then try it on a pair of fibreglass and metal skis, bound to a pair of plastic boots at a speed of 140 km/h (85 mph) over bumpy terrain on an icy mountainside. This is the fastest possible position on skis.

It isn't easy to hold a good tuck on the hill, and racers are rarely in an optimal position. Clean aerodynamic positioning of the body, countered by the physical movements needed to ride a fast ski down a steep, bumpy mountainside sets up a conflict for the skier which is the true technical challenge in downhill racing. There are several variations of the optimal position, all designed to accommodate terrain and to keep the racer smooth and fast. However, it is essential in all

by permission of F.M.H.

Steve Podborski is airborne as he executes a high-speed turn through a transition at Schladming. He looks well ahead to prepare for changes in terrain.

positions that the skier keep the elbows in and the hands up and together, which in turn pulls the shoulders together into a streamlined shape. This offers the least frontal surface and gives the racer the impression of cutting through the air like a wing. The feet should be spread to the approximate width of the shoulders and the weight well centered on the skis for stability. The ski poles are kept tight to the side of the body, and follow its line.

When large arm movements are necessary for balance or driving through a turn, skiers should always keep their hands somewhere within the periphery of their vision. If at any point racers cannot see their hands, they are too far to the side or back, which can lead to total loss of control when travelling at high speeds. This rule of thumb may seem to give skiers a lot of leeway, but the harder they are concentrating while racing down the hill, the narrower their field of vision becomes. They are continually being forced to drive their arms further and further forward.

Riding the Ski

People can reach a higher velocity on skis than they can in a free fall from an airplane. Although snow friction exists at the interface between the base of the skis and the snow surface, it causes far less resistance than wind or air friction. Specially prepared bases and waxing help to reduce snow friction even further. While in the tuck position, a downhiller will attempt to keep his skis as flat as possible on the snow surface, because the metal edges are much slower than the prepared bases of the skis. The skier will also attempt to keep his skis on the ground as much as possible: air time costs time and directional control is lost when the skier leaves the ground. A good position is easier to hold on the ground, and even irregular terrain can be travelled faster on the snow than in the air. One way to keep skis on the snow surface is to absorb bumps and moguls by relaxing the legs so that they absorb bumps like pistons. Stiff-legging it into a mogul slows a skier down considerably, because the skis will leave the snow. This method of tackling a bump will be discussed in greater detail in the section entitled "The Suck".

by permission of Salomon

David Murray keeps his weight on the downhill ski — crucial in any turn for beginner and expert alike.

Zimmerman

Michael Veith of West Germany shows good basic technique, although he is edging a little too hard and his weight could be further forward over his skis.

Zimmerman

Switzerland's Walter Vesti is over-rotated and sitting back, which causes the tails of his skis to slip out. The lack of snow flying out from behind him indicates that this turn is not being carved.

The Turns

The most important thing to remember in making a great downhill turn is the same thing an instructor will emphasize with any beginner: keep the weight on the downhill ski. This is the key to all good turns. It cannot be stressed enough.

Making a good downhill turn is not simple, so it follows that making a great downhill turn, one that is faster than all the competition, is much more complex. Imagine the difficulty of carving a turn on a frozen pitch so steep that you could not walk up it and so icy that even an excellent skier could not free ski down it. This slope is the length of a football field and as hard as a hockey rink. There are three control gates along it, forming an S-turn. Downhill racers reach the first turn at a speed of 110 km/h (68 mph), the second at 120 km/h (75 mph), and the third at 100 km/h (60 mph). The last turn will bring them to a long flat section of the course. At the bottom of the pitch there is a large net to protect them from hitting the trees, should they fly off the course.

This S-turn section of the course takes only five seconds to ski. Five seconds! On a two-minute course! To make this section count, the skier must execute it with close to technical perfection. The winner will have to have had a perfect run.

At the top of the pitch, the racer attacks the turn. Timing at this point is crucial. A perfect downhill turn is as accurate as a fine pencil arc drawn with a precision instrument on a piece of white paper. If the skier moves into the arc too soon, he will be high and risk crashing into the control gate at the middle of the turn. If he moves in too late, he will be too low in the middle of the arc, and risks missing the next gate. Valuable seconds will be lost while he recovers his position.

When anticipating a turn around a control gate, the skier begins to rise slightly out of the tuck, while shifting his weight forward and rolling onto the downhill ski. At the same time, the inside edge of this ski is secured. The motion must be smooth and continuous. The racer must roll, not jump, or he could be blown right off the course: there is tremendous wind resistance at a speed of 120 km/h!

As the edge is set, the downhill knee reacts to absorb the shock created. This knee leans into the hill. At the same moment, the skier angulates his upper body over the lower ski in the direction of the turn, keeping both hands forward and the inside arm up.

by permission of F.M.H.

David Murray, his weight well distributed over his skis, rises slightly from his tuck and rolls into a turn at Val Gardena. He looks to the side in anticipation of a change in direction.

A turn executed with the least possible sideslip is a *carved* turn. In a perfect turn, the skier has applied just enough weight to the inside edge. If there is too much weight on the downhill ski, it will chatter and speed will be lost.

It is actually possible for the downhill skier's speed to increase out of a turn, and he may, in fact, leave the turn at a higher velocity than that at which he entered it. To do this, he moves back slightly on his skis and releases the weight from their tips to stop the skis from carving. At the same time, he must get quickly back into the optimal tuck position.

It is on steep sections of the course such as these that racers attempt to build up speed, which must then carry them across the flats. When coming out of the last turn before the flats, they must be very careful not to hit the edges too hard, or they will be unable to maintain their speed over the long flat section which follows.

sequence by Jalbert Productions, reproduced by permission of Salomon North America

1. Canada's Dave Murray becomes airborne off the Hausbergkante (a sharp drop off on Kitzbühel's Hahnenkamm). He is anticipating his landing and looking in the direction of his turn.

3. The course turns into a transition which ends in a compression upon landing. At the same time, Dave begins to roll into his turn.

5. Murray becomes extended once again off a long roll in an attempt to keep his feet on the snow for speed and control.

2. Murray becomes fully extended in preparation for the shock of landing.

4. After initiating the turn, David moves his upper body and knees in the direction of the turn, lifts his inside foot and places his weight on his downhill ski to hold the edge.

6. Landing off the roll on this difficult transition section of course, Murray stands high to absorb the impact of the next bump while maintaining a long carved turn.

1. Canada's Ken Read is off his line at this point on the Hausbergkante. After hitting a patch of ice he was forced too low on his turn. The tracks of Franz Klammer, who had the same problem, are also visible.

3. Read lands on the same spot as Franz Klammer, instead of rolling to the left as Murray did in frame 3. Ken must roll slightly to the right in order to get into the proper position. (David Murray — frame 4)

5. Off the first roll, Ken extends his body to correct his position through the transition.

2. Just landing, Ken takes into account his position and looks in the direction he must go to regain seconds lost by his mistake in line.

4. Ken begins to make his left turn and widen his stance in anticipation of the rolling terrain (transitions).

6. Upon landing, he shifts his weight over his downhill ski and begins the turn to the left.

7. Well forward and in a strong, balanced stance, Dave carves his turn over this section. The snow is softer here, melted by the strong sunlight.

8. Murray gets air time off the roller (transition). He keeps his arms well forward and because of his angulation, the ski bases become visible.

9. Just landing, Murray drives hard with his outside arm to prevent his skis from sideslipping on this fallaway turn.

10. Regardless of speed, the racer's weight should be properly distributed in a carved turn. The spray from David Murray's downhill ski is evidence that his weight is in the proper place over his downhill ski.

11. The terrain drops off again and David extends to absorb it. For balance, his arms are apart but forward, well within the periphery of his vision and he rides the ski properly to the end of the turn.

12. After completing the turn, David begins to move back into the tuck position as he approaches the Zielschuss.

7. Ken must turn much harder than David Murray at this point, to correct his line.

9. Ken is carving well on his skis as he lands off the roll, but is still trying to correct his line.

11. Read is 'jamming at the gate' slightly in trouble. He must drop his arm to avoid hitting the post.

8. He goes into a 'strength move', shifting his weight hard onto his downhill ski and keeping his arms forward to give him added rotation in the turn.

10. Ken approaches the end of his turn.

12. Ken is losing time here: instead of moving into his tuck, he is still turning hard to maintain his line.

Olle Larson, James Major

A great downhill turn is a personal experience and comes with hours of practice. Each racer does it slightly differently, but the greatest turn is always the fastest one. There are no points awarded for style, but the fastest turn is the result of simple economics of motion.

The Pitches

If there are no control gates on a pitch, racers are "egging it" — tucking it out! There are no significant turns to contend with, only bumps, ruts and roughness. It is here that skiers must build to the greater speeds which will carry them across the flats, and small mistakes cost valuable seconds. When racers talk of mistakes on the pitches, they are talking about breaking from a tuck or sometimes doing what feels safest and most secure, instead of what feels fastest. Even with bumps, ruts and roughness, good downhill racers will hold their tuck down the steepest, meanest and fastest pitch in the world. And they will be sure to choose the very fastest line. In downhill racing, as in motor racing, the fastest line is not always the shortest one. Skiing the fastest line through the various control gates often requires maintaining a line within as little as a few inches from the gate or a mark in the snow. Quite often it becomes obvious that it is fastest to follow the route of earlier racers down the mountain. This means attempting to ski within half a meter of a distinct track over the three-kilometer course.

It is here on the pitches and across the flats which come after them that the Canadian Men's Downhill Team earned their reputation as the "Crazy Canucks", the "Kamikaze Kids".

David Murray approaches one of the crucial turns at Niagara, Lake Placid.

As he sets the edge, his downhill knee reacts to absorb the resulting shock.

He angulates his upper body over the lower ski, always looking in the direction of the turn.

The knees are the driving force in this well-carved turn. David applies just enough weight to his inside edge: too much weight causes chattering skis and lost time.

The Flats

The so-called flats on a downhill course compare in slope to an easy or intermediate hill. An average skier "tucking out" even through these sections, would find it quite an experience indeed!

Nevertheless, the transition from the steep pitches to the flats subjects the racer to incredible G-forces. When the facial skin starts to stretch, he knows he's arrived.

Skiing the flats requires the same precision as skiing the rest of the course. Races can be won or lost here and speed can actually be gained through this section. Success on courses with a lot of flats may depend to a greater extent on equipment and choice of wax, but the clever downhiller, with his technical expertise, can use the flats to advantage.

A racer who rides a flat ski, a "good slider", is the fastest competitor here. In a slight turn, he is light on his edges, since metal is so much slower than the waxed composite base of the ski. But there is more to success than just standing well on the skis. In order to carry the speed built up on the pitches, the skier must keep a tight, compact tuck position, with his weight slightly to the back of center on the skis. He must be totally relaxed and able to absorb the bumps. A racer who loses on the flats has generally lost the race. The best downhillers in the world make few mistakes here and this is one spot on the course where human error factors are negligible.

Coaches and ski companies will usually use the flats to take section times during training runs. It is also on the flat sections where crucial decisions regarding the choice of skis and waxes are made, based on the data provided by electric timing of runs.

Every racer executes a downhill turn slightly differently. David Murray (top) points in the direction of his turn with his right hand and keeps his left hand high. Ken Read (center), also pointing in the direction of the turn with his right hand, keeps his arms well within the periphery of his vision. Steve Podborski (bottom) keeps his inside arm low as he begins the rotation needed to bring his ski around.

by permission of Shell Canada Ltd.

Zimmerman

Steve Podborski flies off a pre-jump at Lake Placid in near perfect form. His hands could be slightly higher and more in front of his body.

Zimmerman

Canada's David Murray seems relaxed enough while airborne after a Lake Placid pre-jump, but his open position may have cost him the victory at the pre-Olympic trials, in which he placed third.

The Pre-Jump

All downhill courses traditionally have large bumps along their terrain. Without preparation for these bumps, the skier would be hurled off into space at speeds up to 140 km/h. Pre-jumping is a technique used by the racer to absorb a bump at these high speeds. Although it would be foolhardy for recreational skiers to attempt a similar manoeuvre while skiing flat out on steep terrain, they can begin practicing on a flatter slope or over a familiar bump.

Prior to running the course, the racer carefully inspects each section, making a mental note of where all the bumps occur, and planning well in advance how to tackle each one. Lack of commitment when approaching a bump is probably one of the main causes of casualties in downhill racing.

When he approaches the bump during a run, the skier takes air just before reaching the lift of the bump. This leap minimizes the air time and prevents him from flying off the bump, usually to disaster. High speeds are what make pre-jumping tricky and dangerous. The skier must anticipate the exact moment at which to open up and push off the ground before reaching the lip of the bump. The distance at which the downhiller leaves the ground before the jump depends on how fast he is travelling. This distance increases with speed, and so does the danger.

As a racer approaches the pre-jump, he

Although Ken Read of Canada is in an excellent tight, compact position following this pre-jump at Lake Placid, his arms could be slightly more forward for further streamlining.

Austria's Ulrich Spiess has developed an unconventional position — arms held high and at his side. Although his body position is slightly open, Spiess appears to be well balanced and confident in the air.

rises from the tuck position, while at the same time pulling his heels up towards his seat. His forward motion allows him to absorb the bump by actually jumping over it. He leaves the ground and sails over the ledge of the bump, immediately resuming the tuck position, both for safety and to avoid slowing down. With his upper body, he shifts his weight forward in an attempt to keep his back parallel to the steepness of the pitch on which he is about to land. While in his tuck position in the air, the racer's perspective is all horizon and sky: once he has left the bump, he cannot see the part of the hill where he will land. The timing of the racer's take-off must be perfect. That is the only way to be sure that he will land safely. If a downhiller pre-jumps too early, he will land on the top of the bump and fly right off again. If he pre-jumps too late, he will fly off the lip of the bump into space. Re-entry is disastrous. If he pre-jumps with more push coming from one leg than the other, he will approach his landing sideways.

The only way to pre-jump is properly. Smooth. Fast. Compact. Perfect.

The Suck

In some situations, racers will prefer to remain on the ground and "suck" a bump. Instead of leaping before they reach the bump they will stand up out of their tuck and absorb it with their legs. Sucking a bump doesn't require the precision timing of a pre-jump, it is much less dangerous, because the chance of being propelled off into space is greatly minimized, but it is also much slower. Generally, skiers will suck a bump only when they have no time for a pre-jump, or occasionally if the bump is not too large.

Dean Colour

Canada's Mike Irwin has missed the timing of his pre-jump and finds himself sitting too far back and slightly out of control.

Riding Bumps

The third way of tackling bumps on the downhill course is to stay in the tuck and ride them. Sometimes a coach will advise his skiers to egg it right over a series of small bumps and hold the tuck that won't quit, no matter what! Downhillers will ride bumps which are small enough not to throw them too far. Sometimes, unfortunately, this is the only way to take bumps, because there is no time to set up in order to take them in any better way. Hopefully, however, a racer will be sure that this is the fastest and most efficient way to get across them.

THE RELAXED ATTACK — CONQUERING FEAR

To get to the bottom of the downhill course, a racer has to make important decisions under highly stressful circumstances. The best and easiest way to make any decision is in a relaxed state of mind. If the racer makes the wrong decision, he can fall and be badly hurt. Fear makes him stiff and tight. Stiffness makes him slow. But the goal is always speed, and the fastest way to ski a course is to attack.

In other sports such as swimming, equally as competitive and psychologically intense as skiing, competitors are in little danger of physical injury during the course of their race. There is terrific demand made on ski racers to attack a fast and dangerous downhill and stay relaxed while doing so. They are often asked, "How do you deal with such high speeds?" or "Doesn't going that fast scare you?" Their most common response would be, "Not afraid, nervous perhaps, but not afraid". Certainly it would be good cause for terror for the average skier to subject himself to the demands of a World Cup calibre downhill course. How is it possible for racers to look at the Streif at Kitzbühel, the most difficult and treacherous course in the world, and calmly consider the fastest way down?

Fear is not conquered overnight. But by the time a racer is capable of winning a World Cup, fear of moving fast has virtually disappeared.

Experience is paramount to the conquest of fear. Each run down a training course should be a learning experience. No skier feels fear as long as he is skiing well within his limits. Fear only exists when these limits are being extended, during momentary losses of control, when the skier is forced to meet new challenges. As the ability and confidence of a skier increase, he begins to realize exactly what his limits are, and when and where risks can be taken to expand them. It is while taking these risks that new reactions and new and better ways of coping with as yet untried situations are developed.

However, it is not enough just to have skied many runs over many courses. Each new course presents its own challenges and a racer must work hard at eliminating all fear of the unknown. It has been said and proven time after time that a

by permission of Shell Canada Ltd.

Steve Podborski "sucks up" the lip before a steep pitch at the Shell Cup Championships, Lake Louise, Alberta, 1979.

downhill course always looks tougher at first than it is. A racer carefully inspects and studies each course before he ever runs it non-stop, memorizing each bump and analyzing each turn. His plan of attack is prepared long before he steps into the starting gate. Once the limits of the skier and the course have been explored during training, he moves into the race fully aware of the possibilities and his potential to win.

A skier's coach plays a significant role in increasing confidence and thereby diminishing fear. The coach's responsibility is to prepare a racer to meet new challenges, while not pushing him unreasonably beyond his capabilities. It is just as terrifying and dangerous an experience for an unprepared racer to get in over his head as it is for the average skier. But the racer has his coach to rely on for seeing that transitions to new plateaus are made at the proper pace. Once a skier has competed successfully at one level, he will have the confidence to move on to the next.

It is easy to see that this same kind of progression is the most successful way for recreational skiers to improve their performance on the slopes. Moving too quickly and getting in over their heads will only lead to discouragement and possible injury.

One of the most significant recent changes in ski racing circles has been the technological advance in equipment. These developments have resulted in greater control of the skis at high speeds and changes in technique which have given the skier more confidence in dealing with speed.

There are other elements of fear which exist in all highly competitive sports, dangerous or not, and which must be conquered by all successful competitors. The fear of failure and defeat and the fear of a foolish mistake cause pre-race nerves and jitters at all levels from the most elementary to the most advanced.

"Psyche" is the state of mind of confident winners, developed by performance under pressure. It is what helps them overcome the fear of defeat and enables them to attack relaxed. It is what enables them to rebound mentally after a fall or close call in training. It is what makes them get back into the starting gate as if nothing had happened after bruising or breaking body and ego at 120 km/h.

When the top fifteen racers finish within one second of the winning time over a two-minute downhill course three kilometers long, it becomes evident that something more than just training and technique are making the difference.

by permission of Molson Breweries of Canada Ltd.

More and more recreational skiers are participating in organized races, in which they compete against their own best performance.

TIPS FOR THE RECREATIONAL SKIER AND YOUNG RACER

The same sound basic technique which is used to ski deep powder snow is also used to ski hard-packed snow or ice, such as is usually found on a downhill course. Skiing is a difficult sport to master because, unlike most others, conditions can change daily and terrain is always varying. But skiers cannot be considered to have mastered the sport until they can ski under all conditions.

It is not the intention of this book to be a basic instructional manual. However, the average skier taking note of these tips from some of the top downhill racers in the world will be well on the way to mastering the sport of downhill skiing.

1. Learning

If the skier choses to learn to ski on his own, instead of taking organized lessons from a professional, there is a great deal to be gained from watching and imitating the technique of more advanced skiers. Ski racers and their coaches spend many hours studying videotapes of their competition and comparing the relative merits of executing a turn or taking a bump in many different ways.

To build a strong foundation, the skier should concentrate on one skill at a time, beginning with the weakest, until it becomes second nature.

2. Equipment Maintenance

Racers have many advantages over recreational skiers, long before they ever reach the top of the mountain. One of the most significant of these is that their equipment has been carefully maintained. Any skier can share this advantage by paying attention to his own equipment, especially his skis, and servicing it whenever necessary.

Bases The base or running surface of the ski should be filed flat. A concave or convex running surface makes turning very difficult. All skis should also be hot-waxed every eight to ten skiing days to make them run faster and turn more easily. This is particularly important when skiing in heavy, wet or new snow conditions. Scratches and gouges, especially those in the area under the boot, which make it almost impossible to sideslip properly, should be repaired immediately.

Edges Ski edges must be sharpened regularly, so that they will continue to cut the snow in a turn. Most ski shops will repair and service skis, but many minor repairs, waxing and filing can be done at home by the skier.

3. Warm-up

A good warm-up on the first run of the day can help a skier's performance for the whole day. Most racers begin by taking their first run very slowly. They take long, wide turns and concentrate on relaxing. Gradually they build speed and make shorter radius and higher speed turns. This helps to build confidence and is a useful progression for the recreational skier to make as well.

4. Body Position

The recreational skier should always assume a natural, erect body position when skiing. He is forced to bend his knees slightly by the forward lean in his boot, but most skiers tend to hunch over or bend too much at the waist. The body weight, instead of being over the balls of the feet, where it ought to be, is then too far forward, and turning becomes much more difficult than it need be.

This position is modified for a beginning racer, who should nevertheless not start out in the full tuck position. He will be slightly lower and more compact than usual, to gain stability through lowering the center of gravity and speed by

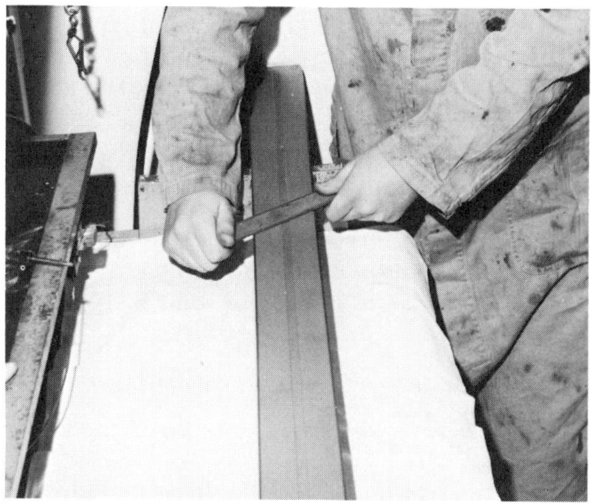

Flat Filing

Scraping the base smooth after repair work

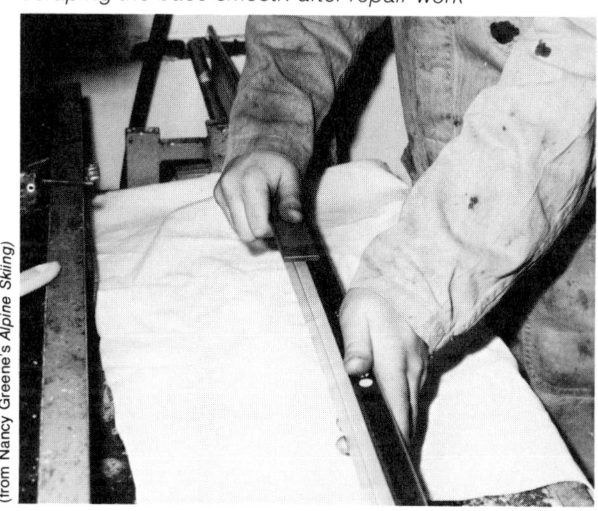

(from Nancy Greene's *Alpine Skiing*)

Side Filing

Fred Mullane

Unweighting is done by raising and lowering the body through the ankles and knees. Some unweighting can be done through the hips, but this is not as effective and the skier risks a fall like the one above.

streamlining. Ankles and knees are flexed forward, the waist is bent slightly, shoulders pulled together and hands are held low and together.

5. Stance

The skier's feet should be kept comfortably apart. This allows maximum balance and the ability to recover in time from potential falls. Many skiers strive to keep the feet locked together and the skis locked into two straight running tracks. This is unnecessary, and the points gained for style will soon be lost when the skier falls. A reasonably wide stance also allows each leg to work independently and the weight to be kept on the downhill ski. It is important to feel the skis flat on the snow, allowing them to wander and weave, not riding on one edge or the other.

6. Arm Position

The chief function of the arms in skiing is balance. They should never be locked into position, but held loosely and comfortably, ready to react quickly in any unanticipated situation and move with the rest of the skier's body. Through a turn, the arms co-ordinate the upper body with the lower. They should be kept as low as possible, comfortably to the side and in front of the hips at all times throughout the turn.

7. Turning

In order to be able to turn successfully in all snow conditions it is helpful to understand the mechanics of a turn. Skis are designed to turn as a result of changes in weight distribution throughout their length. Because skis are narrower at the waist than at the tip and tail, they have a curved running edge. If a skier sets his ski on this curved edge by bending his downhill knee forward and into the hill, and applies pressure to the middle of the ski through the arch of the downhill foot by pressing the shin against the boot tongue, the ski will carve a smooth arc across the hill. In a properly carved turn, the skier speeds up, while remaining in complete control of his movement.

8. Knees and Ankles

The skis should always be controlled through a turn by the knees and ankles. Lateral movement of the knees into the turn holds and controls the edges. The ankles move with the knees in a slight rolling motion into the hill, the direction of the turn.

9. Unweighting

Unweighting is the upward movement of the body, which reduces the weight over the middle of the ski. This motion is necessary to turn or change direction. A skier coming out of one turn and going immediately into the next will accelerate as he unweights off the original controlling downhill ski. The powerful up-motion will briefly increase the pressure on the edge and cause the ski to carve more sharply.

The unweighting should always take place through the ankles and knees. In some cases, such as over deep ruts or big moguls, unweighting can be done by raising and lowering the hips, but this is neither as effective nor as efficient. It is also very dangerous, because once a skier is committed too far, he cannot recover. He will hook the inside edge and fall into the hill. While it is even possible to turn the ski by pivoting the entire body

Fred Mullane

The actual turning of the skis is done through the feet. Abbi Fisher, shown at the lightest point during the unweighting process, properly uses the center of her boot as the pivoting point in the turn.

Angelo Cavalli

during the unweighting, it is not as fast or as accurate as pivoting through the feet and lower body. The upper body should therefore be kept as stationary as possible. At slow speeds, unweighting is very important and can become quite an exaggerated movement, with the inside ski sometimes coming right up off the snow, although this is not imperative. At high speeds, however, the centrifugal and gravitational forces, along with the speed, make it almost unnecessary to unweight the skis consciously.

10. Feet

The actual turning of the skis at the lightest point during the unweighting should be done with the feet. They should turn so that the skis pivot through the center of the boot. This movement is quite simple and can easily be practiced while riding up the chairlift, to get the feel.

Fast does not mean out of control. Werner Grissman carves a fast, controlled turn. His outside leg is the workhorse, carrying 90-100 per cent of the load.

11. Pole Plant

The pole plant sets the timing for the unweighting motion. The pole should be planted at a comfortable distance in front and to the side of the ski boot. There is no need to reach for the point where the pole is to be planted. At the same moment as the pole is planted, the lateral force of the lower body (knees and ankles) should be used to release the edges and begin the unweighting motion. The skis should begin to come around and the weight is shifted to the downhill ski.

The force of the pole plant is relative to the skier's speed. In a downhill race, the pole does not even touch the ground, whereas at slower speeds, it must be quite firmly planted.

12. Anticipation

Most skiers could improve their skiing by twenty to thirty per cent if they would concentrate on keeping their eyes well ahead. Most skiers tend to watch the terrain just in front of the tips of their skis, but one section of the course leads quickly into the next. At 30 km/h (20 mph) the eyes should be focussed fifteen to twenty meters ahead. As the skier increases his speed, he should be looking forty to fifty meters ahead. The skier should also occasionally glance further down the hill to make sure that there are no major problems ahead, for which he ought to be preparing himself.

13. Speed

We all have a little race car driver in us when we sit behind the wheel, a little Jimmy Connors in us on the tennis court and a little Henri Duvillard on the ski hill. That little voice inside says go faster, reach farther, ski harder — me against the mountain! Go for it!

To ensure the mountain doesn't win the confrontation, recreational skiers or young racers can learn a few secrets that will stack the odds in their favor.

- Going fast does not have to mean out of control.
- A long radius, carved turn is both faster and more controlled than a skidded turn.
- The outside leg in the turn is the workhorse, carrying ninety to one hundred per cent of the load and it is the carve control.
- Upper body movements are quiet and subtle, but very important in reinforcing holding power.
- Motion on the snow is faster than in the air.

Skiing fast adds a whole new dimension to enjoyment on the slopes. But skiing fast, out of control on any hill can be a terrifying experience which might result in injury. Opt for speed with control using long radius carved turns as a starting point. Choose terrain carefully when you "go for it" the first time. Select a slope of gentle to medium steepness with even terrain until you are used to the sensation. Don't endanger yourself or others by skiing all out when slopes are crowded.[1]

[1] Used by permission of Ski Canada magazine.

PLANAI
parmalat
3
SCHLADMING
1
2
3
FISCHER

CHAPTER THREE

Equipment

The ski equipment used by the downhiller is highly specialized and sophisticated. Research and development in racing equipment are carried on with one major goal in mind: maximum speed with minimum risk. The Lauberhorn downhill in Wengen is now being run in 2 minutes, 35 seconds, compared to 3 minutes, 5 seconds ten years ago.

Recreational skiers may feel that this has little to do with the equipment they are likely to find in their local sporting goods store, but ski racers are the test pilots of the ski industry, and developments in their equipment generate significant changes and improvements in all equipment for skiers at all levels.

SKIS

Skis are the most important piece of equipment for the racer, and vital to the success and enjoyment of any skier. They are precision instruments, and special attention must be paid to their construction. Racing skis are similar to the top model recreational ski, but more time is invested in their construction. They are handmade of the best woods, glues and metals available. Because of the fierce competition involved, any significant technological breakthrough becomes the manufacturer's closely guarded secret.

Height, weight and fitness information is stored by manufacturers on the amateur racers to whom they supply skis. Test teams work year round in all kinds of weather, in all conditions from very wet to very fast, to get each racer the right skis. Fischer, for example, tests from 4000 to 4500 pairs of skis each season. About 700 of these are then made available to the racers they supply.

Length

Most downhill skis range from 221 cm to 225 cm, whereas recreational skis are normally only 130 cm to 195 cm in length. Anyone familiar with the "Short Ski Progression" or "Graduated Length Method" of learning to ski will realize that only a very advanced skier would be capable of successfully manipulating skis of 223 cm — almost twice as long as the skis that an adult might learn on! It is amazing that such a long ski can turn with very little effort at speeds ranging from 5 km/h up to 140 km/h.

Tips

Downhill skis worn by members of the Canadian team are built with a hole the size of a tennis ball sculptured into an extremely flat tip. This flat tip improves the flex characteristics of the ski and hence its turning and sliding capabilities. While it makes the ski easier to handle, the flat tip is also

by permission of Salomon

The tips of downhill skis are very flat to improve their flex characteristics. The sculptured hole in the tip reduces the ski's mass, making it less bouncy on rough terrain and easier to turn.

much more susceptible to breakage and therefore impractical for the recreational skier.

The mass of the ski tip is reduced by the large hole which makes the ski less bouncy on rough terrain and easier to turn. Unfortunately, there is always the danger that in broken snow conditions, chunks of snow will shoot up through the hole and hit the skier in the face at 120 km/h. Thank goodness for goggles!

Sidecut

Every ski is wider at its shovel and tail than at its waist, or middle. The sidecut is the curve formed along the side of the ski because of this change in width. The greater the sidecut, the less the ski needs to be put on edge, in order to make the same radius turn.

Recreational skis have a relatively large sidecut, as do slalom and giant slalom skis. This natural arc allows the skier to get the same turning action with less effort. Downhill skis, on the other hand, have a much smaller sidecut. There are two important reasons for this. First, a large sidecut tends to make the ski too turny or "nervous". Unless the terrain were perfectly flat, the ski would constantly be turning from underneath the racer, making it difficult to hold a perfectly straight line of attack. Second, too much sidecut causes drag: there is a significant snowplow effect from the waist to the tail.

Over the years, sidecut has been altered drastically, in order to achieve optimum turnability and slideability. Through computer testing, the most favorable sidecuts for downhill, giant slalom and slalom events have been determined. Recreational skiers can now choose the sidecut which is most appropriate for the kind of skiing they prefer.

Flex

Flex is the degree of bend in various parts of the ski. In general, stiffer skis are needed by heavier skiers and are preferable for hard, icy surfaces, whereas softer skis are used by lighter skiers and in powder snow conditions.

A ski becomes progressively thicker, and hence stiffer, from about 15 cm behind the point of contact of tip and snow to the waist, just beneath the ball of the foot. Towards the tail of the ski, the process reverses and the ski becomes gradually thinner and more flexible. While an even flex of tip and tail is usually recommended for most recreational skiers, those who are more advanced often prefer the tail somewhat stiffer than the shovel area. The downhill race ski, however, has a proportionately much softer and more flexible tip, although the ski itself is always much stiffer than any recreational ski.

The flexible tip allows the ski to ride easily on new snow and not plow clumsily through it. In addition, if the ski is too stiff towards the top, the skier would have to shift his weight too far forward to turn and would be thrown off balance.

Although a ski that is too stiff is difficult to turn and will not hold an edge no matter what a skier does, a reasonably stiff ski will slide better because the weight of the racer is distributed more evenly over the running surface. A compromise between slideability and turnability must therefore be reached in the racing ski.

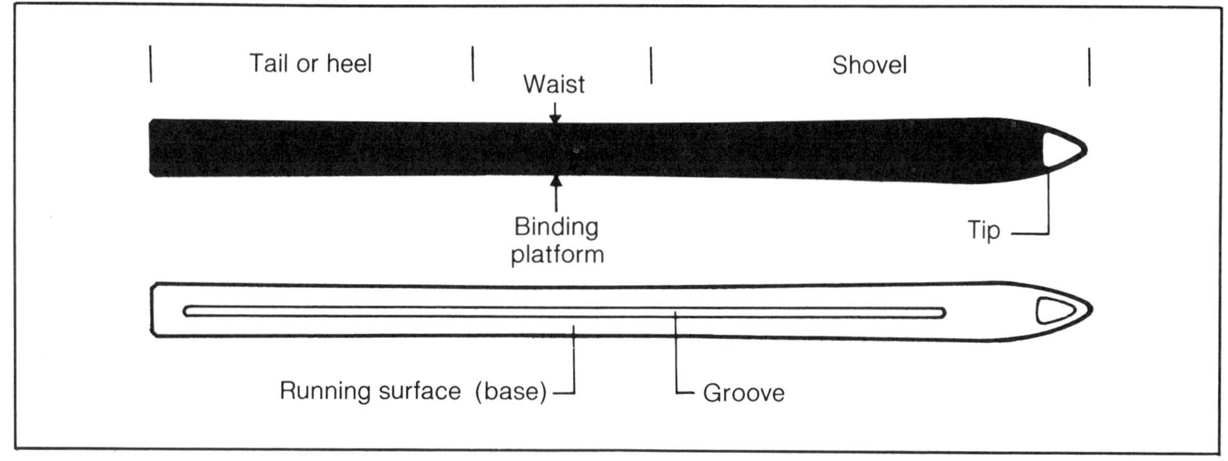

(Alpine Skiing)

Running Surface

The running surface has been the most carefully researched part of the ski in recent years. It consists of the base and the edges. A groove runs down the center of the running surface, allowing it to run fast and track straight.

Edges The metal edges of the ski hold it steady through a turn, acting as a blade cutting through the snow. The edges of downhill racing skis are extremely narrow. Metal travels slowly on snow and racing edges are now about 1/3 as wide as they were just five years ago. On training skis that have been used solidly for a month, the edges get so thin from constant tuning that they actually peel off like tinsel. Thin edges, while absolutely necessary to minimize the effect of drag, definitely shorten ski life.

Bases It used to be that racers, like recreational skiers, would use their best pair of skis to perform in any and all conditions. Five years ago, research began on matching bases to various snow conditions. Freshly fallen snow is very different from snow which has melted and then refrozen, or artificially made snow. Racers can now select from up to six different polyethylene bases the one which best suits the snow conditions. However, snow at the top of the course is often radically different from snow at the half-way point or the bottom of the course. Specialization mustn't be too great, or racers will find themselves caught. At the World Cup in Crans-Montana, Switzerland in 1978, for instance, David Murray was in fortieth position after the first twenty seconds of the training run, but finished that same run with the best overall time.

With six different ski bases to choose from, the racer needs six pairs of racing skis, which are used only on race day and for only one run. Six duplicate pairs are also needed for use in training runs. Usually there will be yet another pair of skis on hand with the most commonly used base (the one for a hard-packed, almost icy course) in case the racer wants to make two training runs on the same base-type ski during one day. After each run, the skis are returned to the technician for waxing, sharpening and flat filing. Finally, the downhiller has a pair of warm-up skis, which are used for inspection of the hill or free skiing on runs open to the public. Altogether, that makes fourteen pairs of downhill skis that must travel with each racer around the World Cup Circuit. The "ski man" or supplier/technician also has spare skis ready, in the event of breakage or damage to the bases. One good scratch on the base of a ski makes it useless for racing. Increased friction at the scratch slows the ski down. The damaged ski is repaired and demoted to training status, and a new pair must be brought in for the race.

Race skis are used only on race days, and then only for approximately 2 minutes. However, because of the precision with which these skis are made, the fact that a skier has never actually trained on the race ski is not a problem. Each ski with the same base type turns almost exactly as all the others of that type. This is essential because

by permission of Shell Canada Ltd.

the racer often makes two training runs and one competition run in a day, necessitating the use of three different but identical pairs of skis.

Skis are continually being tested to aid the development of new and faster bases for all conditions. In this testing program, carried out on a small glacier in the Austrian Alps, five men ski run after run, straight down a hill, through a series of electronic time traps, five days a week, all year round. Testing is stepped up when there is a demand for a new type of ski to meet a particular set of conditions. During the season before the Olympic Games, testing teams are sent to the ski site to develop a new ski expressly for use there. For example, artificial snow, as is primarily found on Whiteface Mountain, Lake Placid, site of the men's downhill at the 1980 Olympic games, has very compact ice crystals. The surface is hard and granular. A specifically developed ski base matches these snow conditions and anticipates the weather conditions expected in Lake Placid in February.

The premature release of a binding at high speeds can lead to serious injury. Racers and recreational skiers alike must check bindings carefully prior to a day's skiing.

BINDINGS

Bindings serve two functions. First, they make possible the transmission of the skier's body motion through the boots to the skis. Second, they eliminate as far as possible injury caused by falls. Racers, just like recreational skiers, occasionally make errors, which make it necessary to part company with their skis on short notice and at high speeds.

Top-of-the-line bindings, such as those used by downhill racers, are very sophisticated in design. A binding must be light and uncomplicated, yet keep the boot in contact with the ski while incredibly strong and variable forces

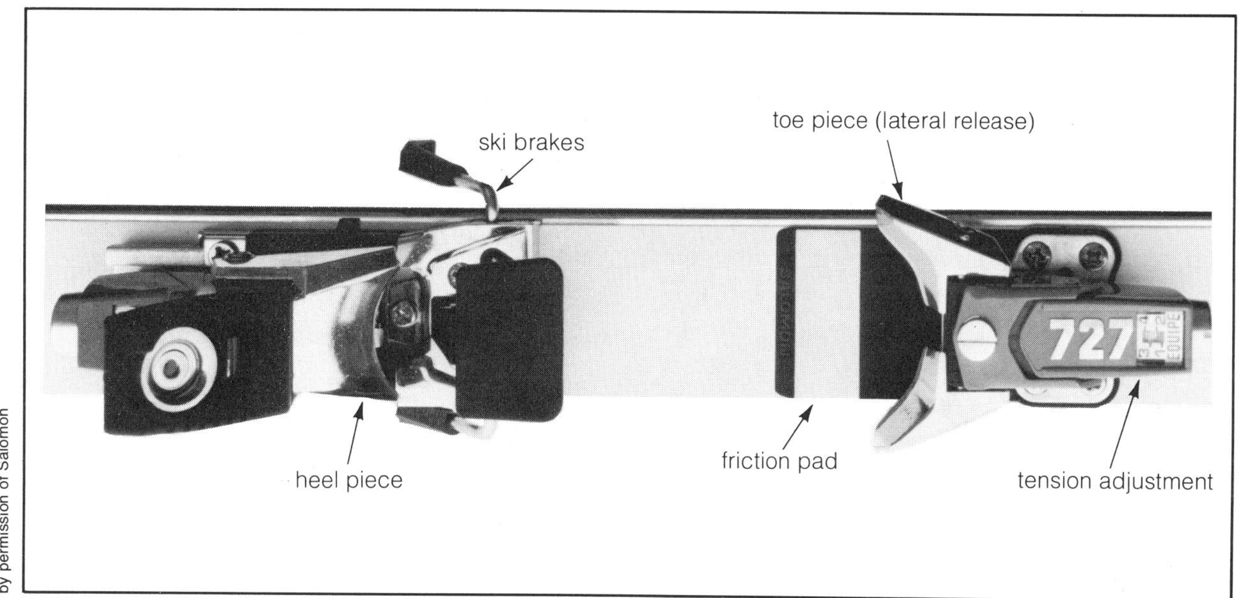

by permission of Salomon

The Salomon 727E "The Competitors' Choice"

are acting upon it. The forces which are applied to the binding, and subsequently the leg, are torsional or twisting, lateral and bending forces. There is much more stress on the torsional properties of the binding, but in the event of possible disaster, the binding must release in any crucial combination of forces.

There is a great deal of controversy surrounding the choice of bindings. For downhill racers and recreational skiers, it is primarily a matter of which binding they trust, though all should have two-way release — forward and lateral — which will function if there is too much twisting pressure. Modern bindings are all very effective, but in order to function correctly, they must be properly adjusted according to the manufacturer's direction. In general, physically stronger and more advanced skiers may have tighter settings than those who are less proficient. Most ski shops have machines which will indicate the correct setting for any skier's needs or level of expertise, and the staff will adjust them accordingly.

Racers, in particular, must rely on a binding to hold on through the fastest and roughest sections of the course, when they are going full out. Otherwise, they may tend to ease off in a turn, thereby losing valuable seconds, for fear that the binding will kick out with the jarring or centrifugal force of the turn.

Racing bindings are the same as those sold to all skiers, except that far heavier springs are used. These make the bindings much harder to release, because the demand placed on them by a racer is so much greater.

The other great difference between racing and recreational bindings is the absence of a safety strap or runaway device on a racer's ski. These are absolutely necessary in a public ski area where the possibility of injury to a fellow skier from a flying ski is very great. However if a ski remained attached to a skier falling at a speed of 140 km/h (85 mph), very serious injury would result.

Before every training run and race, bindings are finely tuned to ensure that the forward pressure is balanced with the lateral settings. Recreational skiers should also inspect their binding settings and major moving parts daily. Settings may change because of vibrations from skiing or transporting. Before leaving the ski shop with new bindings, be sure to get a detailed explanation of how they function and how they should be checked.

No World Cup racer would ever put on a ski when there was snow on the bottom of his boot. Bindings should be set to hold a boot as snugly as possible, and any snow creating gaps between boot and ski could cause the binding to snap open unexpectedly.

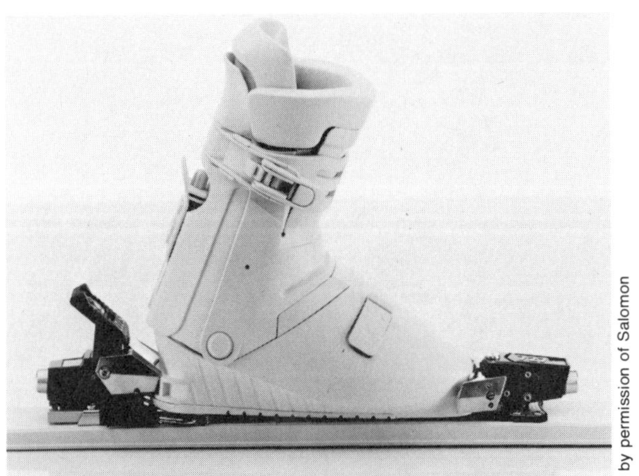

This ski boot, a new prototype developed by Salomon, provides good support while still allowing forward flex.

The plastic balls on the ends of downhill ski poles are far more aerodynamic than baskets and act as feelers against the snow.

SKI BOOTS

The evolution and development of ski boots has been particularly dramatic over the last fifteen years. Boots have evolved from nothing more than a very stiff leather lace-up hiking boot to the new plastic breeds with buckled systems, which give optimum support and comfort. The original plastic boots were very stiff and low to the ankle. Gradually they grew higher, until some were midway up the calf. Today, ski boots are slightly lower and of varying stiffness.

The main design consideration in a ski boot is that it provide good lateral support, while allowing for comfortable forward and minimum backward flex. This forward pressure is considerable for any skier, but even greater for racers. A softer forward flex in the boot absorbs bumps more easily and allows more forward lean, so that they can get into their low tuck position. During the fall training, the racer's boot, custom-made to suit personal preferences, is often shaved down from its original mold to make it softer in this forward bend.

On the other hand, the boot must still provide good support so that the racer can hold the ski on its edge through a turn over the hardest ice. For this reason, racing boots have much stiffer sides than recreational ones.

The natural standing position of some people prevents the soles of their boots from sitting perfectly flat. By "canting" or wedging the edges of the boot soles, the normal stance can be corrected, ensuring that the skis rest perfectly flat on the snow. A flat ski is much faster, because there is no drag effect from the slow metal of the edges.

POLES

Whereas poles may be only a minor part of a recreational skier's equipment, they are essential to a downhill racer.

Ski poles are made from metal alloys, which are very light, yet have a high tensile strength and remain tensile at very cold temperatures.

The downhill racing pole, which is the same length as a regular pole, is bent about half-way along to conform closely to the skier's body when in a low tuck position. Erik Haker of Norway is the only downhill racer still using straight poles. This particular development in downhill equipment is one of the few which has no practical benefit for recreational skiers.

Plastic balls replace the baskets fastened to the end of regular ski poles. A recreational skier will plant the pole in the snow to help initiate a turn. The baskets prevent the pole from sinking too deeply into the snow. Downhillers are moving much too quickly to plant their poles. Instead, they use them much more as feelers and for balance going into a turn. The balls have a much lighter touch, and are far more aerodynamic than baskets.

Zimmerman

Erik Haker of Norway, the only racer on the circuit who still races downhill with straight poles, takes a Lake Placid jump.

Lindley photo

Read and Irwin, clad in warm-up suits during course inspection, wear new helmets with collapsible foam suspension systems. Read (left) also wears a detachable face guard.

CLOTHING

Helmets

Helmets are relatively new to the ski racing scene and are still used only in downhill. They have developed from a simple leather construction to a sophisticated apparatus with a collapsible foam suspension system which absorbs shocks and blows. Some manufacturers are even beginning to introduce face guards, which are usually removable because they are often distracting and sometimes cause goggles to fog up.

Although there are many different brands of ski helmets, all have two features in common. First, they are cut high at the back to enable the racer to keep his head up and see where he is heading while in a low tuck position. Second, they are very lightweight, since the forces acting on the racer are severe. A heavy helmet would greatly hamper his speed and movements.

Goggles

Goggles are essential to the racer and useful to any skier. If the racer cannot see where he is going, he isn't going to get there. The frame, slightly modified to fit perfectly into the helmet shape, is black, which helps to minimize reflection, and lined with foam rubber to give a comfortable, air-tight fit. Prior to each race, new lenses made of laminated plastic, and treated with chemicals to prevent fogging, are inserted into the frames. Lenses come in three colors: polaroid blue for sun, green for medium brightness and yellow for snow and fog.

Suits

The suit worn by downhill racers is skin-tight and one piece, with all seams sewn in the back for maximum streamlining. Unlike the recreational skier, whose main concerns when choosing a ski outfit should be warmth and freedom of movement, the racer must think first of speed. In the sixties, racers tied their pants at the knee to stop them from flapping, and travelled at correspondingly slow speeds: 90 km/h maximum. Suits began to change when the Italians introduced a rubberized version, with a thin rubber coating, overlaying the cloth. These were incredibly fast through the air. As Italians began to win consistently over more experienced and technically better racers, the rest of the skiing world began to take notice of their innovations. Unfortunately, when the Italians fell, they didn't slow up, but went blasting down the hill, often straight into the trees or off the edge of a cliff. The FIS, whose job it is to safeguard the racers against unnecessary injury, outlawed these so called "fish skin" suits.

Undaunted, the manufacturer reversed the material, putting the rubber coating on the inside. These, too, were very fast through the air, but racers felt as if they were skiing in a sealed plastic

courtesy of Gameplan Information Office

The service "rep", like the Formula I mechanic, is responsible for equipment maintenance.

bag. They perspired heavily while skiing down the course and froze while travelling up the lift to the start of the second run. Once again, the FIS stepped in and outlawed these suits. They then established an arbitrary standard of fifty litres of air, which must pass through one square meter of material per minute (50L/m²/min.), in order to ensure that all suits breathed properly. This rule caused one of the biggest upsets in World Cup downhill history during the 1978-79 season. Canada's Ken Read was disqualified at Morzine, France after a spectacular first place finish, because he was wearing a new and unapproved suit, which, when tested after the race, did not meet this minimum permeability requirement. Luckily, teammate Steve Podborski was there to take over first place from him.

Since this new ruling was made, manufacturers have been attempting to find a material that comes as close to the limit of permeability as possible and yet is as fast as possible through the air. In addition to satisfying these requirements, the material must be elastic and move with the racer's contortions. Various synthetic fabrics, specifically developed for use in ski racing suits, have now replaced the rubber in earlier suits. These new suits are even faster than the old, and are much more comfortable. comfortable.

While these suits are very effective windbreakers, they are not warm enough for the recreational skier, and racers must wear warm-up suits until just before the start of a run.

Gloves

For most recreational skiers, mitts are the best protection for the hands. However, racers prefer less bulky gloves, which will not affect their control or their feel of the poles. Like ski mitts, they are padded to protect the racer's hands from weather and ice abrasions.

SERVICE MAN

National ski teams on the World Cup Circuit are surrounded by other people whose services are indispensable to their success. One of the most important of these is the ski service man or rep. Like the mechanic on a Formula 1 driving circuit, he is responsible for the fine tuning and maintenance of the racer's skis, a duty which recreational skiers must perform for themselves. (See Chapter Two: *Tips* for ideas on equipment maintenance.)

Aside from waxing and flat filing the racing ski bases, tuning the edges razor sharp and filling gouges and scrapes, the rep acts as a liaison between the skiers and the manufacturer. He chooses the skis, both training and racing, from the factory, and joins the coaches in making decisions on waxing and choice of ski bases for a particular race.

One of the major headaches for the rep is the team's wax room. This is where the skis are filed, scraped, cleaned, waxed, sandpapered, brushed and generally pampered. It is usually a storage room in the basement of the hotel, but can be anything from a hotel room to a garage or service station.

This room has to be big enough to lean a minimum of 30 pairs of skis along the walls without punching holes in the ceiling. It must also have space to set up a work bench for skis 223 cm long. The temperature should be approximately 20°C (68°F) to allow easy waxing. Last of all, it should be accessible. Stairs and turns are tough to handle while carrying 13 ski bags with six pairs of 223s plus the coaches' and staff's equipment, all weighing . . . too much.

Harvey Soicher

Modern Ski Technology: Canadian Downhiller David Murray

ELECTRONIC EQUIPMENT

The US and Canadian Ski Teams work together with electric timing clocks, taking section times along the course during training. With three or more of their own units set up along the course, as well as the official course and section timing system, the teams can get a very accurate idea of where time is lost and should be made up. Times are also taken in the race itself, to help coaches determine who to watch to discover the best line and maybe get some technical clues. Skiers will often travel through as many as thirty light beams on their way down a course.

Each evening after training, at least an hour is spent analyzing these section times and the video-tapes done along with them. In the first runs, the video is set up on the toughest turn. Then, after the team has some times, it is set up on the sections of the course which seem to be causing problems for the members. This use of video has done a great deal towards advancing technique in modern ski racing.

A good performance in alpine skiing is the result of a combination of factors. Technique, coaching, training, physical condition and personal attributes are all essential to success. But modern ski racing has become so technologically sophisticated that skiers must take advantage of the best equipment available if they want a chance at walking away with a World Cup Gold.

CHAPTER FOUR

The Training Process

Overall downhill performance is a function of technique, equipment, physical condition, coaching, and training.

Some racers are fortunate enough to be born with natural strength, others with a keen sense of balance and flexibility. Although everyone is born with individual strengths and weaknesses, all successful racers must have realized the importance of perseverence in maintaining long-term, intensive training programs. Serious competitors must devote at least one and perhaps two hours a day, year round, to physical conditioning and training. They must also do morning and evening exercises which normally take from 10 to 15 minutes. A successful racer, or any accomplished skier for that matter, has had to learn to make the best use of his strong points. But eventual success comes from hard work and training that go far beyond any mere raw talent.

To get maximum results in any training program there are certain rules which must be followed. Before starting intensive exercise or working with weights the trainee should begin each session with a good 5-minute warm-up of stretching exercises such as touching the toes, running on the spot, skipping, jumping jacks, light jogging or stride jumps. The serious competitor must train daily: short daily training periods are better than one long session per week. It is important to concentrate on individual weaknesses and not spend too much time working on strong points.

PHYSICAL CONDITION

The following elements of physical conditioning are necessary for good performance on the slopes: strength and muscular power, endurance, stamina or resistance, speed or mobility and flexibility.

1. Strength and Muscular Power

Because the rigors and demands placed upon the downhill racer are so great, strength and muscular power are the most important elements of physical conditioning and consequently require the most training. A person who is physically very strong should be able to learn to ski faster than a less powerful individual, but hard work will show results for everyone.

Strength is the ability of a muscle to overcome resistance. At high speeds, the resistances are particularly great. Skiers need strength in the upper legs and midsection of the body. They must have strong quadriceps, hamstrings, adductors, back and abdominal muscles. The downhill racer with power in these muscles is better off than a skier with endurance in these muscles.

Steve Podborski warms up for his daily training session with skipping exercises.

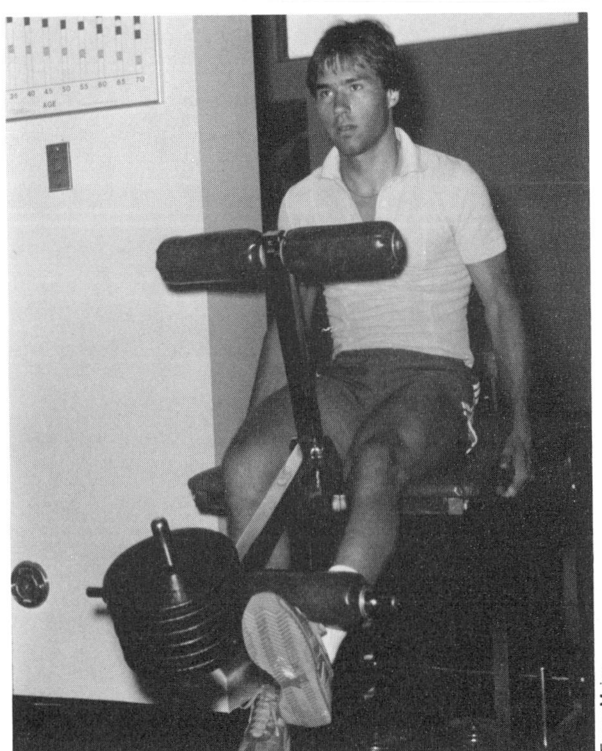

Podborski uses training equipment to build strength in the quadriceps, the muscle group used most extensively in skiing.

Muscular power is the ability of a muscle to produce a force quickly. Fast reactions are more important in alpine skiing than heart and lung (cardiovascular) strength, which is the key factor in cross-country skiing.

The easiest way for a skier to develop the necessary strength and power is to ski vigorously on a regular basis. Since this is impossible on a year-round basis, the competition skier must substitute daily training activities.

Although this year-round training program is not necessary for recreational skiers, they too should participate in some strength-building activity in the off season. Strength will make skiing easier and more pleasurable. October is a good time to begin some sort of exercise program to prepare for the ski season. Cycling or hiking in the mountains with a pack is excellent exercise to stimulate the muscles used in skiing. Calisthenics and isometrics are also useful in developing strength and muscular power.

The serious skier must do all of the above, and participate in a weight training program.

WEIGHT TRAINING

The skier's weight training program is designed to pay particular attention to increasing strength in primary muscle groups used in skiing. These are the muscles of the upper legs and midsection of the body: quadriceps, hamstrings, adductors and abductors, back and abdominal muscles. Weight training improves both skeletal and muscular power and allows the skier to assume the correct body position more easily while practicing technique. Besides developing strength, the skier's weight program includes a specific regimen to develop endurance. The racer alternates the three regimental techniques (for strength, power and endurance) using the same set of twelve exercises throughout the week. Each workout should be no longer than 45 minutes.

Certain basic precautions should always be taken when using weights. Each exercise session should be preceded by a long and thorough warm-up and followed by a cooling-off period. A warm muscle is less susceptible to strain and a cooling-down period prevents stiffness and

Power Press

Side Jumps

Trunk Rotation

Side Benders

Bench Steping

3/4 Squats

Toe Raises

Franz Maier

Trunk Rotation with Arms Extended

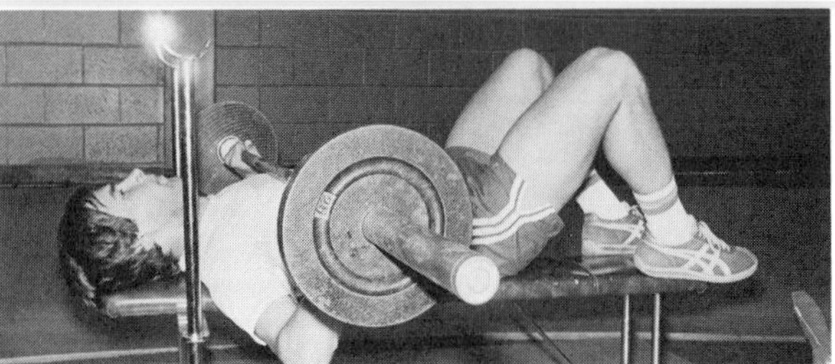

Franz Maier

Bench Press

promotes mobility. Correct lifting position is also important. The motion of lowering the hips should be done by flexing the knees while the head is kept erect and the back remains upright. The trainee should use correct breathing procedures, inhaling when executing a movement and exhaling when returning to start position.

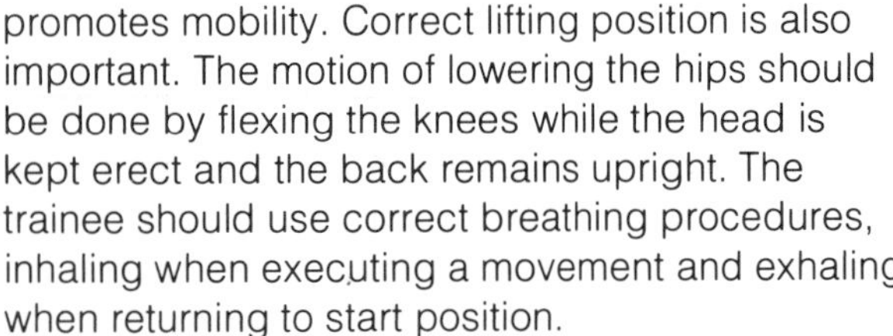

Power is a combination of strength with explosive force. Weight training for muscular power is done by decreasing the number of repetitions of a particular exercise while increasing the load (the amount of weight). The ideal load to produce maximum power is 60% of the athlete's maximum lifting ability.

Set	Load	Repetitions
I	60% of maximum lifting ability	6
II	75% of maximum lifting ability	4
III	90% of maximum lifting ability	2
IV	100% of maximum lifting ability	1

To train for muscular endurance, the athlete attempts to reduce local muscular fatigue and improve the quality of work performed over the duration of the workout. He performs each exercise with the weight poundage at 50% of his maximum lifting ability. Keeping the weight constant, he repeats the exercise as many times as he can. At each workout for endurance, preferably twice a week, the athlete should attempt to increase the maximum number of repetitions.

Muscular strength refers to the intensity of muscular contraction. The maximum weight poundage for this type of training should be 60% of the athlete's maximum lifting power. He should perform three complete sets of exercises with 4 to 6 repetitions of each exercise. The weight is increased for each set and the number of repetitions is decreased.

Each year members of the Canadian ski team undergo laboratory testing to determine their fitness capabilities. Specific strength testing is done to evaluate both the current strength performance of the athletes and the effects of training programs in progress. This evaluation is important in establishing the athlete's current status so that direction can be provided in the design of strength training programs. Strong, well-developed muscles are not only resistant to injury themselves but also provide protection to joints and bones.

2. Endurance

Endurance is the ability of the body to supply oxygen to the muscles (aerobic) when producing an effort and to sustain this effort over a long period of time. This is where good cardiovascular capabilities come into play for the recreational skier. A skier should be able to enjoy a whole day's skiing from morning until afternoon without becoming overly tired. However, as there is no obligation to ski non-stop for any length of time, he should stop and rest when he feels the need. With low endurance, it would be difficult for a skier to ski two or three consecutive days, and by the fourth day performance would undoubtedly suffer.

Although a downhiller's performance is not as reliant on endurance as it is on strength, a racer must be able to sustain run after run of downhill training and cope with rigorous travel schedules. A training program on snow can run up to five consecutive weeks, and racers must sometimes travel 12 to 14 hours per day by car or put up with racing within days or even hours after inter-continental flights. Only a skier with high endurance will be able to benefit from this long-term training.

Jogging and cycling on a regular basis are probably two of the most beneficial forms of exercise to develop endurance for both recreational skiers and competitors. Interval training and circuit training are also used by the competitor to build up endurance levels and develop cardiovascular capabilities.

RUNNING

Skiers benefit from a program of running that combines jogging for warmup, wind sprints, long strides and easy running. Cardiovascular development and ankle and knee joints are all strengthened by a running program done on soft turf. Pounding hard surfaces such as concrete and pavement can cause damage to those complex knee and ankle joints.

CIRCUIT TRAINING

Circuit training combines a number of successive exercises. The racer progressively overloads and increases the work which is customarily done by the muscles. The sessions of exercises are done without resting between and the timed circuit is repeated three times.

Franz Maier

Steve Podborski practices short sprints, simulating the speed and low position of downhill racing.

To establish the number of repetitions of an exercise, the athlete first does as many repetitions of each as possible in one minute. He records the number, rests for one minute, and repeats the procedure with the next exercise. The training dose of repetitions should be half the maximum number of repetitions. For example, if the participant performs fifty repetitions as his maximum, then twenty-five repetitions should be the number done in training.

Circuit training is a self-competitive exercise, with the participant trying to improve the time for completing the whole circuit. It is not recommended that anyone undertake this exercise program without supervision and medical advice, unless he is accustomed to vigorous exercise.

Bench Step — Stand in front of a bench or ledge. Step up with the right foot and then the left. Step down. Repeat.

Push Ups — Start from a prone position and push up by extending the elbows. Lower the chest to the floor and return to start position. Repeat.

Lateral Jump — Jump laterally across any line on the floor as fast as possible, keeping feet together.

V-Sits — From sitting position, raise both feet simultaneously until 'V' position is reached. Reverse to starting position.

courtesy of Gameplan Information Office

Members of Canadian ski team free ski in Chile. Free skiing is one of the best ways to train co-ordination, reflexes and reactions.

Hip Raisers — Lie on back with arms at sides and bent knees. Elevate hips as high as possible and then lower to the floor.
Trunk Extension — Lie face down with fingers interlocked at the back of the neck. Raise head and shoulders as far as possible from the floor.
Sprinter — Start in sprinter position on blocks, with one foot straight back and the other flexed with the knee pulled under the chest. Reverse knee under chest. Repeat.
Burpee — Start from a standing position with legs straight. Squat with hands on floor and extend legs backward. Reverse procedure back to squat position and finally to upright position.

INTERVAL TRAINING

Before beginning, the skier should do general warm-up exercises, which increase the heart beat to about 120 beats per minute. He then runs a distance of, say, 200-250 yards in 40-42 seconds. For maximum benefit he should repeat this run 6-10 times, with one minute of complete rest or easy jogging between repetitions. This exercise should bring the heartbeat to 170-180 beats per minute. The heart should not require more than 30 seconds to return to 120 beats per minute, or the level of exertion should be reduced.

3. Stamina or Resistance

Stamina is an element of conditioning quite different from either endurance or strength. It is the ability of the body to produce an effort without utilizing oxygen (anaerobic) and to sustain the effort for as long as possible without a decline in the level of performance. The importance of stamina to performance in downhill skiing is second only to strength and muscular power. A downhill race runs two minutes: two minutes and twenty seconds is a long downhill race. It requires maximum effort by the racer for the full duration of the course. For the recreational skier, the demand for maximum effort is less, and stamina is therefore not so crucial. If he experiences an oxygen debt, he simply stops and rests. This the competitor cannot do.

Approximately 10 seconds after leaving the starting gate racers lose their ability to perform with 100% efficiency. Their bodies begin to build up an oxygen debt which increases as they make their way down the course. As they cross the finish line their reactions, reflexes and co-ordination are greatly diminished and their strength spent. Winners have developed the ability to ski the course while under these conditions of oxygen debt and still maintain maximum effort. The downhiller who has good power left after one minute and fifteen seconds stands a much better chance of finishing among the top ten, despite any technical errors which might have been made.

Exercises for increasing stamina and resistance include circuit training, interval training, running uphill, skipping rope, weight training using light weights, bicycle sprints and training with a maximum weight load for short periods of time.

4. Speed and Mobility

Speed is the ability to execute a movement rapidly. Mobility is the ability of the joints to move with ease. Free skiing is the best way to train one's co-ordination, reflexes and reactions, which are all part of speed and mobility.

Most good racers ski fast and stay in control most of the time. When a skier experiences only momentary losses of control, he is skiing at the proper level. It is during these momentary losses of control that he develops and improves new reflexes and reactions and learns to anticipate the unexpected.

Franz Maier

Podborski runs an imaginary slalom course to develop speed, mobility and co-ordination.

The skier can train during the pre-season for speed and mobility in dry land training on mountain slopes, by simulating the body movements made in skiing. After running up the slope to develop endurance and strength he runs down, jumping and hopping over obstacles. He must stay in a low crouch position, hold back his body weight and keep his stance wide to develop balance.

Gymnastics, short interval running, reaction exercises and short sprinting also help develop a skier's speed; running an imaginary obstacle course through a park or forest, working on a trampoline, or doing floor exercises and gymnastics will greatly improve mobility and co-ordination.

Franz Maier

Podborski demonstrates exercises designed to keep hamstrings flexible. It is important for the racer to do stretching exercises, both as a preventive measure against injury and to avoid stiffness after training.

5. Flexibility

Flexibility is the range of movement about a joint. It is especially important for a ski racer to remain flexible around the major muscle groups to prevent injuries.

Development of flexibility is more important as a preventive measure than to improve performance, although it is a great help to the racer's speed and mobility. He needs particularly good flexibility in his neck to allow him to remain in a low tuck position and still see forward with helmet and goggles on his head. It is also important to do easy stretching exercises to avoid any stiffness which could affect performance.

As part of the Canadian downhillers' physical laboratory testing program, flexibility is measured by a device called the Leighton Flexometer. The purpose of this testing is to measure the skier's increase in flexibility following training segments.

The following exercises are designed to maintain flexibility around the basic muscle groups. The average skier would benefit from yoga or stretching exercises like those in the morning exercises suggested and described in *The Threat of Injury.*

HIP FLEXORS

Begin by standing in a stride position (one foot in front of the other). Sink down and place your hands on either side of the forward foot. One knee should press against the chest. The rear knee is straightened, pulling the foot against the floor. The hips should not be raised. Repeat the above instructions three times; each time sink the hips until they cannot sink any lower.

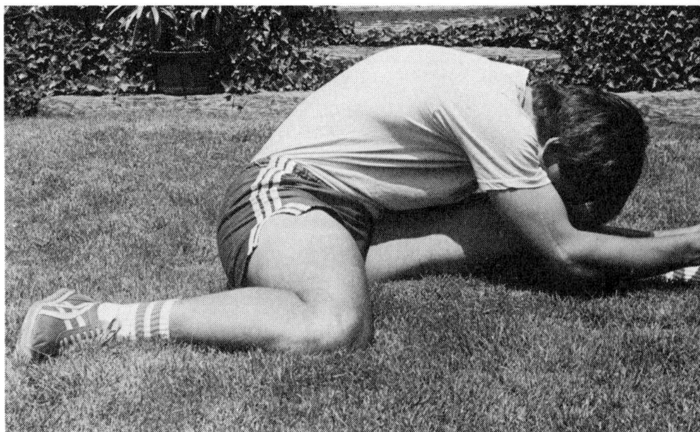

Franz Maier

The hurdle sit keeps muscles of the legs and hips flexible.

HIP ADDUCTORS

Begin by standing with feet wide apart. Bend one knee sideways, allowing the hips to sink down towards the same foot. Pull the straight leg down into the floor. Relax and repeat several times, attempting to sink the hips lower until finally they sink right down to the foot.

HAMSTRINGS

Sit with feet wide apart in front of you. With knees bent, grasp the feet with the hands. Push the heels into the floor, while trying to straighten the knees. Relax and repeat, each time pushing the knees closer to the floor while keeping the hands on the feet. Repeat until knees are straight. Then attempt to touch the nose to the floor between the knees.

HURDLE SIT

This exercise is designed to help hamstrings, trunk flexors and extensors, quadriceps and hip external rotators.

a) Sit with one leg and ankle bent behind you. Then hold the other foot with both hands, bend the knee and straighten the leg, pushing the heel into the floor. Relax, and with knee still straight pull your nose down to touch the knee. Repeat with the other leg.
b) Lie on the floor, keeping the lower back flat. Pull one foot against the seat with one hand and push the knee down onto the floor. Repeat with other leg.

THE TRAINING YEAR

A reporter once asked David Murray, "When does your season end?"

"April 15," Murray replied.

"And when does the new season begin?" queried the reporter.

"April 16," Murray replied.

David Murray was not exaggerating, for during the final races of a season, plans are already underway for the upcoming training year. The training staff begins with an overview of the past season to evaluate the strengths and weaknesses of each racer. Improvements in training methods are thought out, to be implemented in the next season.

The National Alpine Ski Team training program consists of three main periods. During the Preparation period, lasting from June 1 to November 25, skiers concentrate on systematic, rigorous training to further physical fitness in the areas of endurance, power, strength, balance, flexibility and agility.

The Competition Period from November 25 to mid-April is the culmination of dry land camps and on snow training. The athlete is physically, technically and mentally prepared and ready to compete. The emphasis now is on the development of the peak period.

After a long competitive period, athletes have a Recovery Period lasting approximately six weeks, during which time they can relax and heal old injuries. This relaxation time is considered as active rest, in order to maintain proper fitness balance between seasons.

Spring Training

The months of May, June and July give the racer a break from the rigors of travel and the snow. Emphasis is on the development of strength and muscular power. This is a difficult time to train. The winter seems so distant. But it is also a crucial time because during the spring, the skier strives to create a 'platform', a basic foundation which starts him on the road to a maximum level of strength and endurance which will carry him through the rest of the year. He must have the endurance to make the most of training camps in the late summer and fall, when six or seven training runs will be skied in a day. Hours are spent working out in weight rooms or hiking, cycling and running for strength and endurance. By being in peak physical condition he will be more confident and avoid minor nagging injuries such as twists and sprains.

Franz Maier

Running increases strength and endurance. During spring training the athlete creates a "platform" of physical fitness, on which to build over the season.

Franz Maier

Skiers participate in various activities over the summer to develop strength and endurance. Steve Podborski cycles competitively with a club in Toronto.

Summer Dry Land Training

Summer dry land training is a continuation of spring training. Skiers play tennis to develop quick reactions, concentration and endurance, they windsurf to increase strength and improve coordination, they backpack and cycle for strength and endurance. During the early summer, however, more time is also spent on activities that lead to on-snow training. During the months of July, August and September, weight training for strength and endurance continues but gradually changes to emphasize development of stamina.

courtesy of Gameplan Information Office

A group of young Canadian racers assist in carrying equipment up an Austrian glacier during summer training.

Summer on Snow

In late July or early August the first on-snow training for the new season begins. The Canadians generally have a program of two weeks on intensive training, followed by two weeks off. This program extends to the beginning of the competition season. The training, which takes the racer to Argentina, Chile, New Zealand or Australia to take advantage of winter conditions in the southern hemisphere, puts the emphasis on free skiing and technical training in all three alpine disciplines: slalom, giant slalom and downhill. Because shorter radius turns are made in slalom and giant slalom than in downhill, training in them develops the quick reflexes, coordination and balance which are required to ski downhill courses, as well as building strength, confidence and overall good technique.

This seasonal downhill training familiarizes the experienced racer once again with speed. It also trains the less experienced racer to perform at higher speeds. At the beginning, easy terrain is chosen and speed is gradually increased. The training then shifts to more difficult and varied

During the summer, racers train on sun-baked Austrian glaciers as well as in Southern Hemisphere winter conditions.

terrain, which is skied at higher speeds. Emphasis is placed on traverses, jumps and long turns, and practice of the tuck position.

Young racers can develop their downhill skills by performing section training, during which they concentrate on a single task or aspect of downhill racing during each performance time. Between each stage they have a chance to recuperate. For instance, they may take one section of the course in a low tuck position, after which they ski onto a relaxation section of the course.

Continuing downhill, they ski an oblique descent (shallow traverse) then relax, ski through a section of moguls, relax and finish with a section of wide, long, fast turns. As the downhill training progresses, the relaxation stages are shortened until the entire downhill is completed as in a competition.

The young racer can learn much from more experienced teammates, by following and copying their movements down the mountain on slight slopes. Although there is a certain amount of risk involved in following too closely behind another skier, especially at high speeds, a careful racer can learn about choice of line and regulation of speed.

While a great deal of improvement can be made simply by the normal practice of skiing, special training procedures have been developed to help strengthen particular skills and parts of the body. One of these is the use of a long section of rolling terrain on the mountainside.

Various excercises can be done in the fall line, during which the skier concentrates on keeping the upper body as passive as possible during the descent. During an oblique descent, the upper body also remains still, and the skier works at proper weight distribution on his skis. Jumps are practiced to help build confidence and learn correct landing procedures.

Turns and combinations of turns are also practiced and perfected on this rolling terrain. On moguls, skiers can attempt accelerated turns which they must execute without exaggerated gestures, while always keeping their skis in contact with the snow. By making several turns on the rolling slope, each one started on a mogul, skiers develop elasticity and smoothness. During short turns, each one again initiated on a mogul, they can practice gentle knee movement in going from one into the next.

courtesy of Gameplan Information Office

Assistant coach Heinz Kappler gives instructions to a snow-cat operator during training-course grooming in November. The racers' objective in fall training is to get the best run possible in conditions simulating those during a race.

Fall Training

September and October are the most important training months for downhill competitors. They ski hundreds of kilometers in training runs on the frozen glaciers of Europe. On-snow and off-snow training intensify at this time. Run after run on a downhill course allows competitors to work on jumps, aerodynamics, sliding skis on the flats and speed. Confidence is built as training progresses from easier courses to the close simulation of the world class downhill. The search for the perfect run continues day after day. Racers become familiar with the feel of the snow beneath their feet, their bodies react to the speed, and subtleties of aerodynamics are learned.

Emphasis in physical training now shifts in earnest from strength and endurance to the development of stamina (anaerobic training). Increasing importance is placed on mobility, agility and coordination. Conditioning becomes more intensive and more oriented towards specific skiing and racing needs.

November/Fine Tuning

In November, the fine tuning of physical training helps to bring the mind and body to a peak. With the racing season just around the corner, the emphasis is no longer on the quantity of performance, but the quality. The physical conditioning regimen of fall training is continued but the intensity is lessened to decrease the recovery period. At the final downhill camp the racers take only two or three training runs per day. The object is to get the best run possible. Free skiing and giant slalom training for mobility, technique and maintenance of muscle tone are continued. The program builds so that the skiers have reached their peak by the beginning of December.

In the weekly schedule during November, emphasis is placed on physical training early in the week, but by mid-week the emphasis has shifted to ski training. Just prior to the week-end the skier rests. This schedule slowly adapts the body and mind to the schedule followed during racing season.

THE RACE SEASON

The skier's physical and mental functions must be at a peak when the race season begins. He must feel supreme confidence in dealing with the pressures of travel and competition. On-snow training is limited to official training runs and perhaps the occasional giant slalom training run. Physical training is limited to avoid tiring the competitor for competition.

The ski racer must rely on the training of the seven months before the beginning of the season. The hours on and off snow develop the necessary stamina and confidence. With the pressures of travel, the press and competition, the endurance built up in training allows the skier to cope with the extra strain placed on his mental and physical well being.

Leo Mason

The hours of training on and off snow develop the strength and confidence which made it possible for David Murray to recover from this position and place in the top ten at Kitzbühel in 1979.

KITZBUHE

CHAPTER FIVE

The Threat of Injury

Injury poses a constant threat to the ski racer. In its varying degrees of severity it is a problem which can be minor enough to cause only aches and bruises or a missed day of training, or serious enough to cost a life. The speed and the ever present danger of a fall command the attention of millions and make downhilling the most glamorous of the alpine disciplines. However, in the downhill, the most dangerous event in skiing, surprisingly few injuries occur. Thousands of downhill runs are made each year without incident by the world's fastest racers. Nevertheless, with the intense competition and speeds up to 140 km/h, each isolated mistake is a potential disaster.

The FIS ensures that stringent measures are taken to make downhill courses as safe as possible (*see The Downhill*). Before each race is run, a jury carefully inspects the course to see that certain precautions have been taken and standards met. A course which was perfectly safe during training runs can ice up and become very hazardous. At each event helicopters are kept on call to whisk an injured skier to hospital. Medical staff are strategically positioned from start to finish along the mountainside. They are kept in constant communication through a network of two-way radios. Along tricky parts of the course and at the finish, protective netting and hay bales are installed to prevent the skier from hitting the trees or going over an embankment. On the Olympic course in Lake Placid a quarter of a million dollars was spent in protective netting alone.

But for ski racers the best approach to injury is prevention. It is most important for them to keep in good general physical condition. The racer trains to increase strength and endurance and improve flexibility. Specific exercises are done year-round to strengthen vulnerable areas.

Strength and endurance are most important in the prevention of a fall, whereas flexibility is important in the prevention of injury, should a fall occur. Flexibility exercises should be performed as part of any skier's training. A variety of stretching exercises should be included in the racer's daily morning exercises. It really is a good idea for the recreational skier to do light stretching and calisthenics before a day of skiing. A program of calisthenics should begin with neck exercises and work down towards the lower body. Progression of the exercise should be from less strenuous to more strenuous to prevent muscle injury. The following exercises will help to limber the entire body. They

Zehnder

Steve Podborski suffers a chilling high speed fall on the Hausbergkante, a treacherous ledge in the course at Kitzbühel *(p. 64).* *Struggling to regain his balance, Steve hurtles forward at over 85 km/h (top). Blinded by the snow, with his skis travelling in different directions, he plummets further down the slope (center). This fall led to a knee operation, which kept Podborski off the slopes during a painful physical and psychological recovery. The knee must carry the skier's full weight and has little defense against sudden twisting.*

Straddle leans, during which the athlete gradually brings the head down to touch the knee, stretch the muscles in the legs and back.

Lunges build flexibility as well as balance.

should be done 5 times each at the beginning. Repetitions can be increased after each week.

1. *Roll the neck.*
2. *Arm circulation* — Stand with legs apart, stretch arms sideways, and rotate forward and then backward.
3. *Front benders* — With feet together, hands on hips, bend forward then backward from the waist.
4. *Side benders* — With feet together, hands on hips, bend sideways from the waist.
5. *3/4 Squats* — With hands on hips and upper body erect, bend the knees and sink the body until the backs of the thighs are almost resting on the calves. Raise body slowly.
6. *Toe-touching from sitting position* — With legs straight out and arms extended above the head, bend forward from the waist forcing the shoulders down and keeping knees flat against the floor.
7. *Sit-ups.*
8. *Push-ups.*
9. *Straddle leans — Stand* with legs in straddle position, lean forward, grasp the inside of the ankles with the hands. Pull forward slowly while straightening the knees.

For more flexibility exercises see *The Training Process*.

Probably the most common medical problems which the team experiences are colds and minor infections. These ailments, which would keep a person off work for a day or so, can affect the skier's agility and split-second analysis while racing. Minor bruises are also a common complaint. A bruise will not generally force a skier to stop skiing unless it is at the boot top, for instance, caused by the rubbing of a tight boot on the shins.

The most common of the serious injuries are those which occur to the knees. This is a particularly vulnerable joint: although it must carry the skier's full weight, it has very little defence against sudden twisting movements. Its capacity for rotation from side to side is very slight. Should the binding not release in a fall, injuries to the knee can be quick and severe.

Knee injuries can run the gamut from a simple sprain, which takes from one to two weeks to mend, to rupture of the knee ligaments, which requires surgery and six to nine months of physiotherapy to heal. The lack of a team doctor and physiotherapist can lead to improper care of injuries and often make the recovery period much longer.

To prevent injuries to the knee the muscles must be strengthened above and below the joint. Leg exercises involving resistance against heavy

Franz Maier

Poor visibility, bad weather and fogging of goggles can also cause serious falls.

by permission of Molson Breweries of Canada Ltd.

Helmets provide protection against head injuries from minor to major concussions.

weights and isometric contractions of the muscles surrounding the knee are also valuable. To help recovery from knee injuries, exercises are done to strengthen the quadriceps (muscles above the knee). Under the supervision of a physiotherapist, the patient does leg presses, leg extensions and deep knee bends. He gradually works toward weight training with increasing weights. Medication is also administered to deal with the problems of excessive swelling and pain.

The ankle is also a particularly vulnerable area. Injuries to the ankle range from simple sprains to complicated fractures. Jogging, skipping and general strengthening of the leg muscles can help prevent ankle injuries.

Although the helmet offers a certain amount of protection, probably the third most common, and undoubtedly the most severe injuries are cerebral, ranging from minor to major concussions. Shoulder dislocations, cracked or broken ribs, cuts and abrasions, and internal injuries also occur in serious falls.

Often the causes of injury are out of the skier's control. The experienced competitor has worked long and hard to minimize the possibility of mistakes. But nightmares do come true: a skier takes a gate too high and catches a ski tip, hooks an edge at high speed on a flat section, collides with another skier who has strayed onto the course, miscalculates the timing in a pre-jump, or crosses his ski tips.

Poor visibility can also lead to accidents, and bad weather and fogging of goggles have caused many serious falls. Accidents also occur more often for racers with higher start numbers, because courses often become deeply rutted as more and more skiers blast their way down the slope and wear down the track.

Course inspection and training runs are a great help in preventing injury. A certain amount of caution must be exercised during the early runs, until the skier has a good feel for the speed and the terrain.

Entering the final schuss at the Hahnenkamm at Kitzbühel, David Murray threw caution to the winds. "It was during the first training run of the day, and the initial two kilometers of the piste had been flowing quickly and smoothly underfoot. Passing through the "Hausbergkante" and making a good left turn through the transition onto a long steep sidehill, I felt myself gaining speed and decided to tuck it out down the final steep incline leading to the finish. I wasn't fully aware of the upcoming sharp transition and was already in too low a position to absorb it anyway. The resulting crash left me senseless for the rest of the day and generally hurting for some time afterwards. The possibility of doing well in an important race had been virtually wiped out."

Aside from the obvious physical pain of an injury there is the threat of developing a permanent chronic disorder or never being able to race again.

Zimmerman

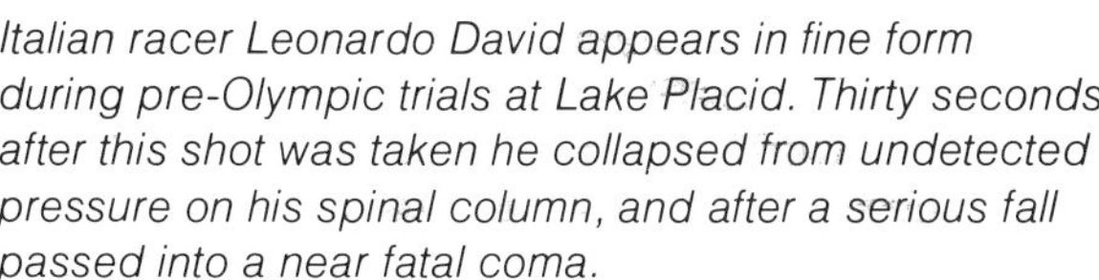

Italian racer Leonardo David appears in fine form during pre-Olympic trials at Lake Placid. Thirty seconds after this shot was taken he collapsed from undetected pressure on his spinal column, and after a serious fall passed into a near fatal coma.

by permission of Shell Canada Ltd.

An ugly example of a fall at a speed that makes snow feel like concrete.

The injured skier is out of the action, and misses the actual competition time, as well as the valuable training miles. It is important to stay within the group to keep on top.

An injury is a jolt to the skier's confidence, which is so vital to his chances of victory. Even after recovery, the psychological damage of an injury remains, and a racer often begins to wonder if the pain and hassle will recur. A skier does not even need to get a scratch to be mentally and emotionally affected by injury. Roland Collumbin of Switzerland broke his back twice, in two consecutive years, off the same double bump, now known as Collumbin's Bump. It affected his friend, Phillipe Roux, so much that he never skied as well again. After Michel Dijon was killed in a training run prior to a World Cup event, the results of his teammate and friend Patrick Pellat-Finet plunged, and he retired from amateur downhill racing shortly afterwards. Franz Klammer, gold medal winner at the Innsbruck Olympics, has also suffered a decline in his results following the accident in a Europa Cup downhill in which his brother, Klaus, was paralysed from the waist down.

There is tremendous pressure, both internal and external, to start skiing again following an injury. Many racers return to the circuit before they have completely recovered. Since they are not in top shape, their performance and results are adversely affected, which in turn is very damaging to their confidence.

No racer or other athlete should return to his sport until he has recovered one hundred per cent. The responsibility for avoiding a premature return to competition, which could cause an injury to become a chronic condition, lies with the coaches and officials in an amateur sport.

If a skier has suffered an injury requiring surgery and a cast, it is best to start from scratch the next season. There is a tendency for racers who are injured early in the season to rush back too soon, perhaps half way through, without total recovery or sufficient training. It is ill-advised for a skier to attempt a comeback for the last few races after suffering a minor injury mid-way through the season. There must be time for complete rehabilitation and then special retraining to get his skiing up to pre-injury level of competence.

Some racers have made excellent comebacks following major injuries. In this long hard road to recovery which takes a person from World Cup downhill to crutches and then back again, a toughness of spirit and determination is instilled in the skier, which can be learned in no other way.

A BIOGRAPHY OF INJURY

By David Irwin

The 1975-76 season was proving to be one of my most successful winters of skiing. After years of advancing through the Pontiac Cup (a ski series for young Canadian racers, sponsored by General Motors of Canada) and Can-Am circuit competitions, I had at last reached the pinnacle of ski competition, the World Cup circuit. Finally it was possible for me to finish consistently in the top few placings. With my World Cup victory at Schladming, Austria, I was vying with Franz Klammer for the number one world ranking.

Then Comes Disaster

I was soon to become acutely aware of the hazards of downhill racing. That winter I suffered the first of my four major downhill accidents which resulted in serious injury. Many people will remember that spectacular crash which occurred in Wengen, Switzerland on January 10, 1976. It was shown on ABC's *Wide World of Sports* in a terrifying slow motion segment. I bounced from the course at over 120 km/h.

Ken Read had fallen at the same spot only minutes before. I slid slowly to a stop, and Ken passed a message over the two-way radios to the anxious coaching staff, "Skis and equipment destroyed, blood-filled goggles!"

I don't know what caused the fall, it happened so fast. But thanks to a superbly organized rescue team, less than 15 minutes after I had pushed from the mountain top on that fateful run, I was being whisked by helicopter to the "Interlaken" hospital. There, I spent eight days with a severe concussion and a fractured rib, as well as facial cuts and abrasions, caused by my smashed spectacles.

The hundred meters leading up to the fall and the hours until I had fully regained consciousness remain a blank. While some people have tried to explain what happened during the tumble, others have said it is best not to know. Even today it is not clear to anyone why I took that plunge. Maybe my goggles had been knocked from my face by the previous gate or maybe I took too tight an inside line around the turn.

An Olympic Effort

Three weeks after the crash at Wengen I was struggling to regain my form for the Innsbruck Olympics. Race officials were aware of the serious blow I had taken to my head, and it was important for me to be completely checked over by a competent medical staff before I competed. Many questioned whether or not I should be allowed to compete in the Olympics because of that head injury, and there was even an attempt by a few people to have me banned from the Games.

The Olympics are the high point in any athlete's career. Many have suffered much in the pursuit of Olympic honors. In 1972 I passed up the Sapporo Olympics in favor of obtaining a top standing in the Can-Am circuit. At the Innsbruck Olympics in 1976 I was determined to try to do my best for the team and Canada. Happily for me, the official okay to compete came after five hours of examination, which included a brain scan and an EEG (electroencephalograph) test, at the University of Innsbruck Medical School.

After weeks of enforced inactivity nursing my injuries, the downhill training runs quickly exhausted me. But in each of us there is a reserve,

by permission of Molson Breweries of Canada Ltd.

David Irwin competes in his first World Cup downhill event at Val d'Isère in December, 1975.

Irwin's dramatic World Cup win at Schladming, Austria in 1975 placed him right on top, vying with Franz Klammer for the number one world ranking.

something to call on when it's really needed. Racing with taped ribs, I placed a respectable eighth.

Unfortunately, this Olympic finish gave me the desire to continue the season. I was not completely recovered and all my energy and stamina were spent. The World Cup Tour came to North America at that point, but I had nothing left to give and finished the season poorly. It was a very personal decision, but if the situation at Innsbruck presented itself again, I would compete again. However, it was a drastic mistake to continue the season after the Olympics. I needed a very long time to regain my health, and as I raced weakly to the winter's end, I picked up many bad ski habits.

Finish Snare

The FIS downhill course at Cortina, Italy in December of 1976 was frozen hard and much slicker for the race than it had been during training. After tucking through the finish line to place fourth, I was unable to stop quickly enough and slammed into the hay bales which protect the fenced-in finish area. I was not the only competitor to do this: skier after skier plunged into the bales and the poorly planned finish area became littered with skis and hay. There were a number of injuries that morning before race officials could remedy the situation.

While cartwheeling over the snow I received another blow to the head. Although I suffered only a minor concussion, it quickly became a problem because of my previous head injury. The season soured. Our team suffered technical problems related to uncompetitive downhill suits and slow waxes.

I did not want to leave the team again but after two weeks of agonizing indecision I finally had to call it quits. The previous season had served as a lesson and I decided it was best to return home to recover fully.

Zimmerman

This shot of the moment of catastrophe was seen around the world. On January 10, 1976, Irwin fell, hurtling out of control at over 120 km / h. Ken Read relayed the ominous message: "Skis and equipment destroyed, blood filled goggles."

Within fifteen minutes of his disastrous fall, Irwin was in a helicopter enroute to Interlaken hospital.

The Worst Was Yet to Come

By fall ski training of the 1977 season I had made a good recovery. October downhill training progressed on the Hintertux Glacer in Austria. My physical and mental preparation for the coming winter had demanded an ever greater amount of summer training, since the previous season had been cut so drastically short. I started to increase my expectations and as I gained momentum I was eager to return to racing.

First out of a newly set course, I flashed around a blind corner on the middle section and discovered another skier. I was travelling 90 km/h. We collided. My left thigh struck him and flipped me over a five meter embankment. After somersaulting several times, I ground to a halt in the powder snow between two outcroppings of rock. I had landed on my back and was dazed and in pain.

Upon my return to Canada, medical examination revealed that my back had two compression fractures. The swelling in my thigh would not disappear, but instead began to show signs of calcification. This calcification bonded my leg so that it was impossible for me to bend it. Physicians advised an operation to remove the calcium deposits and surgery was scheduled for December in Thunder Bay, Ontario. The odds in favor of a thorough recovery from this operation were not great and a return to World Cup competition by the following season was considered virtually impossible.

I decided not to show for the operation, but instead embarked on a determined program to mend my thigh by more natural means. I had to return to competition! For five long months, I worked to get my leg back to health, sometimes spending up to twelve hours a day. I sought the advice of every doctor, chiropractor, physiotherapist and trainer available. I began physiotherapy programs with daily whirlpool baths and massage. I began knee extensions and straight leg raises and gradually began to use weights. Eventually I was able to perform squats with weights.

By Christmas it was possible for me to ski the gentle slopes around Thunder Bay. Skiing seven days a week, I gradually moved from bunny hills to the steeper slopes. As the winter progressed, and I worked my way to heavy training, I noticed a steady improvement in the strength and flexibility of my leg. There are many fantastic people in my home town of Thunder Bay, whom I have to thank for caring for me and helping me with my struggle.

By March I had permission from my doctors to return to the team, in order to test my leg in the last few Canadian slalom and giant slalom competitions. It was exciting to compete again, but I approached these races with low expectations. This was just a test and I wasn't fully prepared for competition. I wasn't even able to finish the first race, and despaired of ever being able to make a return. But the next day I raced again in the slalom event, and came ninth. The remaining Canadian Spring Series proved very successful and I finished each race in the top ten.

Now it was possible for me to say that the injury had been beaten without an operation, although a mass of calcified bone will always be in my thigh to remember it by. The job at hand was to prepare for a comeback to World Cup competition.

Fritz Lauener

One of the few World Cup downhill events in which Irwin competed during the 1976-7 season was at Wengen in January 1977.

Long Road Back

There are many hurdles to cross in the long road back from any serious injury. An injury often has a negative effect long after the physical hurt has been forgotten. The mind tends to remember and dwell on old impressions which led up to the accident. A long time can be needed to overcome the psychological barriers which prevent a racer from skiing relaxed and confident. Confidence must be patiently rebuilt by skiing at a comfortable level, well within one's own limitations. The skier has to *know* he can do it.

To reduce the threat of re-injury and to ski again with confidence, it is important for the athlete to get back to his physical peak, so that it is possible to handle the strain and exertion of skiing.

After spending three consecutive years recuperating and dealing with injuries, I was worried about the time lost not competing in the world's downhills. I had lost a lot of ground in technical practice. I had also lost touch with my teammates and my concentration suffered. If I was to regain my lost position, I would have to work that much harder than all my competition.

In June, 1978, we began off-season downhill training at Copper Mountain in Colorado. From September until November we trained in the European Alps. I began to make headway. If I made a mistake on one run, I would work on it and have it corrected by the next one. I spent long hours with my coaches analyzing videotape in an effort to correct technical errors. The coaches remarked that my mental and physical condition were better than two years earlier, when I had been winning on the World Cup circuit. Long hours of overtime slowly began to pay off. I was winning training time trials. This season the cards had to be stacked in my favor!

by permission of Shell Canada Ltd.

By the end of the 1978-9 season David Irwin was again in form and preparing for the 1980 Olympics at Lake Placid, New York.

Schladming 1978

In 1978 snow came late to the alpine regions of Europe. The opening international competitions were cancelled or delayed. All the alpine ski teams, the Canadians included, were chomping at the bit, anxiously waiting to test themselves after a long off-season of training and preparation. Finally, the alpine valley town of Schladming came through with the promise of a race, and tons of snow from the surrounding mountain passes and farmers' fields were trucked onto the 3600 meter course.

The first training runs at Schladming were about to begin. I was warmly welcomed by Walter Vesti, a Swiss veteran, who approached me smiling and said, "Dave, I'm happy to see you're finally back with us". Some of my training runs went well, although they were not up to my expectations and I did not place in the top ten. But the excitement of World Cup fever was building.

On race day I poled from the start, anxiously wondering if the months of summer rehearsal had been enough. Despite a start number of 39, I placed seventh and was overjoyed: only sixty one hundredths of a second separated me from the leader, after almost two years of absence from the team.

Schladming was the Canadian team's best finish ever, with Ken Read placing first, Dave Murray second, me seventh and Steve Podborski ninth.

My success was short-lived and came crashing to an end in Val Gardena the next week. I had a high start number again. With the sparseness of the snow cover by the time I pushed from the start, the course was rough and bare spots were beginning to appear.

The upper section of the course went well. On the knoll of the last of the three Camel Bumps, a bared rock caught my ski. It shot me forward onto my face and bounced me five meters into the air. I slammed down hard onto the snow. An Austrian coach who had witnessed the mishap commented later, "Today I saw the end of Dave Irwin". I certainly looked like I'd had it: my face was a mask of blood. I had suffered another concussion as well as a severe general body sprain. My left side was paralyzed, my face ripped open as if I'd been the victim of a mad slasher and I'd chipped my right knee cap.

I returned home to Canada. Three weeks later I was back in Europe, competing on the Europa Cup circuit. My back was still in spasms and I was acutely aware of the pain. An operation was also urgently needed on my knee for an old soccer injury, a fractured kneecap which had failed to mend. The knee had started to bother me shortly before Schladming and I was taking injections of cortisone and anti-inflammatory drugs. I was returning to competition earlier than I would have liked. I was not one hundred per cent recovered. But I felt a great need to get back. My previous absence had been so long. I finished the rest of the winter without incident and successfully lowered my FIS standing from sixty-first on the list into the top twenty. That winter of struggle to make a comeback was the hardest that I have ever known and one which I hope never to repeat.

Injuries can devastate a racer's career. After a serious tumble, it's common from him to ask himself, "Is it all worth it?" Some answer "No". The hard work and intense pain are too much to bear. But for others, there is no choice.

Greg Griffith. Reproduced by permission of Molson Breweries of Canada Ltd.

David Irwin chats with an official at Whistler Mountain, British Columbia in March 1979, where the last World Cup downhill of the season had to be cancelled because of dangerous conditions.

Some time ago a woman of about sixty stopped me on the street while I was at home in Thunder Bay. With a long, serious face she pleaded, "Please, David, think of your mother; stop this ski racing". Inside I feel that there is something tremendously important about the pursuit of fractions of seconds and the challenge of the mountain, even if it means risking so much. Is it to represent Canada and my ski team? Can it be the personal rewards? Or is it simply the challenge and satisfaction of being good at something that I work very hard for?

When I ski, I do as well as I possibly can. When I succeed, I'm happy.

CHAPTER SIX

The Downhill

The downhill is "an event in which the racer must demonstrate excellent skiing technique, agility, continuous concentration, marked endurance and physical fitness, as well as courage. The downhill course must be laid out so that it tests the racer in these characteristics by the concentration of many technical difficulties."

The FIS (International Ski Federation) is the controlling body of all major ski events — alpine and nordic — and is comprised of each participating National Association. The responsibilities of the FIS include establishing rules and regulations specific to a particular event, as well as those common to all.

In order to appreciate the nature of a downhill, some understanding of the structure of competition itself is helpful. World Cup, World Championship and Olympic events are the ultimate competitions.

In Canada, lower level races such as the Pontiac Cup, the Shell Cup and the Molson Cup are also FIS-sanctioned competitions. Before any of these competitions are run, the FIS must approve their scheduling, as it does for all international calendar competitions. The complexities of organizing all these events and of coordinating them with events in other countries are immense. All National Associations submit a list of International and National Championship races to the FIS. These are then organized and scheduled through the combined efforts of each National Association's Technical Committee delegates at the annual FIS Calendar Conference. In this way all circuits leading up to and including World Cup can be run without conflict during the year-long competitive season.

To be eligible for participation in international ski events, a skier must have a license issued by his National Association. In Canada, the Canadian Ski Association assumes the responsibility of ensuring all active competitors are licensed through the FIS. In the USA, the U.S.S.A. (United States Ski Association) performs the same function.

Sponsorship and advertising are also the responsibility of the National Associations and all teams have official supplier programs with commercial firms. Commercial markings on equipment are strictly controlled by the FIS, however, and every effort is made to ensure that amateur status rules are not violated. The amount of monetary support a competitor receives, for example, is strictly controlled. The rules governing amateur status are common to all National Associations and are the same as the rules for Olympic participation. Any infraction by a racer causes his FIS license to be revoked immediately by his National Association, in the name of the FIS.

Leo Mason

A Swiss racer steps into the starting gate, flanked by the Race Starter and Assistant Starter.

Safety netting runs alongside the downhill course at Lake Louise. It is the duty of the Race Jury to ensure uniformity of method and safety in every race.

The finish area is completely fenced in to prevent unauthorized entry and allow access to the racers by the press corps.

Strict regulations also exist with regard to doping, prizes, television and film rights. These have been established to ensure the orderly staging of all FIS competitions.

The rules for the organization of alpine events naturally extend to the way the competitions are run. Each race has its own Race Committee and Race Officials. These are the Chief of Race, the Chief of Course, the Chief Gatekeeper, the Chief of Timing and Calculation, and the Race Secretary. The duties of each member of the Race Committee are well defined and each plays a very important role in the running of the race.

The Chief of Race directs and controls the work of all officials. He must have a sound technical background in the operation of a race, as he will chair the team captains' meeting and act as a Jury member.

The Chief of Course is responsible for the preparation of the course in accordance with the decisions of the Race Committee and the Jury. He must be familiar with local snow conditions and terrain.

The Chief of Timing and Calculation is responsible for the coordination of the Starter, Assistant Starter, Start Recorder, Chief Timer, Assistant Timers, Finish Gatekeeper, Chief of Calculations and his assistants.

The Chief of Gatekeepers organizes and controls all gatekeepers. His responsibilities include crowd control, course maintenance and the proper numbering of control gates.

The Race Committee also includes the Course Setter, the Gatekeepers, Medical and Rescue Services, the Race Secretary, the Chief of Course Equipment and the Press Chief. All these officials are chosen and organized well in advance of the first coaches' meeting.

The Jury is a separate group from the Race Committee, although some members belong to both. The Technical Delegate serves as the Chairman of the Jury and as a technical consultant to the Race Committee. The Referee inspects the course, supervises the general conduct of the race and is in the position of authority in case of emergencies. The Start and Finish Referees ensure that the regulations for the start and finish are properly observed. The Chief of Race and Chief of Course also sit on the Jury.

Before the race begins the composition of the Jury is established. Of the two organizational bodies, the Jury, with the Technical Delegate as a representative of the FIS, has the greater power. It is the duty of the Jury to ensure that the race is run in all its aspects according to FIS regulations. This is an excellent system, designed to ensure

Leo Mason

A large electronic scoreboard indicates the finishing times at Garmisch.

Franz Maier

Nancy Greene-Raine converses with a race official from the communications installation. Extensive communications are necessary to ensure the safety and smooth running of each race.

uniformity of method and safety in every race.

One of the first duties of the Race Committee is the installation of the technical equipment necessary in the running of a race. Direct radio or telephone communication is set up between the start of the downhill and the finish. The entire course must be monitored as well, so that immediate communication with both ends of the course is possible, should a racer fall during a run. The race can then be halted and the chance of a fallen skier being hit by the next racer eliminated. These communication and technical installations also make evacuation of any injured racer as efficient as possible. The safety of the racer is the primary concern of both the Race Committee and the Jury, and they will ensure that all these links are operational prior to commencing the first training run.

Because 15 racers often finish within one second of the winning time in a downhill race, electric timing is mandatory. At World Championship and Olympic Games two independently functioning electric timing devices must be installed. To further insure that no times are missed, manual stop watches are also used as a back-up system. At the bottom of the course, adjacent to the finish area, large electrically designed scoreboards indicate the racer's start time, his interval times, and finally his finish time. By staying close to the finish area, spectators can join in the suspense, watching the scoreboard and waiting for their favorite racer to come into sight!

The start area of a downhill is closed off to everyone except trainers, racers, service personnel and start officials. Spectators and press must be kept away from the racers, who cannot be distracted from the challenge ahead.

The racers are sheltered from the weather on top of the mountain by specially constructed warming huts. Start procedure is well controlled by the starter and his assistants. Specific rules determine what constitutes a legal start and seasoned racers have learned to maximize acceleration onto the course without committing any infractions.

The finish area is also completely fenced in and unauthorized entry is prevented either by the local police or race stewards. Racers will move into a separate fenced area for press and coaches, once their run is completed. From here, they can watch other competitors finish, while conversing with coaches and members of press. During the competition, unofficial times are announced and as soon as possible after all runs have been completed, official times are posted and awards presented. But we are ahead of ourselves — there is much that happens before the awards!

Lindley photo

Coach John Ritchie (left) adjusts names on the seeding board at the coaches' meeting prior to the pre-Olympic trials at Lake Placid.

Leo Mason

A slalom racer skis through the last set of control gates at Garmisch. On downhill courses, control gates are set at least 8 meters apart for safety reasons.

The start order of racers is determined by drawing lots in groups. The division of the racers into groups is the task of the Jury, but in World Cup downhill today, the first ranked fifteen competitors are drawn daily to establish their training order, and the rest of the field runs in order of their world ranking. The FIS Points List, which is worked out by the Classifications Committee, is used for the division of competitors. Thus the top seed, the first group of fifteen, on this FIS list, are the most prestigious downhill racers in the world. They are the ones who will run first in a World Cup race. The rest of the competitors will run in order of their position on the current FIS list. (A more detailed explanation of how world class skiers are ranked follows at the end of the chapter.)

During the competitive season, alleged infractions of the rules often result in protests concerning qualification of competitors, the course, the race, disqualifications, timing, false calculation and clerical errors. All of these are examined by the Jury, in which the Technical Delegate carries the decisive vote. Any debate will be resolved prior to the awards presentation.

All FIS calendar international downhill competitions, including World Cup, World Championship and Olympic events, are run only on courses which have been approved by the FIS. This homologation includes a complete description of the course, its name and geographical location, the start and finish points expressed in meters above sea level, the vertical drop expressed in meters, the surface length, gradient, and description of terrain, the number of gates required under normal and exceptional conditions, the normal snow depth and general visibility conditions, wind effects, crowd control possibilities, and evacuation possibilities for injured skiers outside the course. All these aspects must be examined and passed by the Chairman of the Committee for Alpine Courses prior to the use of the downhill area for competition. A description of the communication system, lifts, medical facilities, and a sketch of the entire course are also considered.

Once the downhill area has been approved, the actual course itself must be set. Official Course Setters are nominated by a body of the FIS called the Alpine Ski Committee to set top international events. Course Setters are subordinate to the Jury and set courses on homologated runs, which must have an average speed not in excess of 100 km/h with a maximum sectional speed not exceeding 120 km/h. Minimum drop from start to finish is 800 meters, while the maximum may not exceed 1000 meters. In turns, the course must be 30 meters wide, while the minimum width in wooded areas is 20 meters. The object of a Course Setter is to provide a "piste" which is safe yet technically demanding and fast.

A young French racer tries to improve his FIS points by competing in the Shell Cup, held at Lake Louise, Alberta.

The Course Setter lays out the course using control gates. The number used on a given course will vary, depending on its length and complexity. A control gate consists of two red flags, each 1 meter wide and 0.70 meters high. Gates are aligned along the racing line, with the two flags at least 8 meters apart. These gates determine the route a racer must take down the mountain. The Course Setter closely monitors their placement on bumps, the proper setting of turns, and makes sure that the competitor can see from one gate to the next as he descends.

It is also the Gatekeeper's responsibility to check that each racer passes between the exterior and interior flagged poles which make up a gate. Any poles knocked down by a racer must be reset in exactly the same position, which has been inked with dye in the snow prior to the race. Gatekeepers also control crowds, maintain the course, and report to the Jury concerning protests and disqualifications. Each Gatekeeper submits his record of the passing of racers to the Chief of Gatekeepers prior to the announcement of the official results.

Once the course has been set, competitors begin their inspection of it on the first training day. The duration of inspection, usually one hour, is determined by the Jury and is a time of concentrated planning on the part of the athletes. They side slip from gate to gate, establishing the line that they will take on their first training run.

Except in the case of a "force majeure", the official training period lasts at least three days. All facilities must be completely prepared as for racing, and official training times are usually taken on the second and third days. If any major atmospheric changes alter the condition of the course, further inspection of the course by the racers is mandatory. Generally, racers inspect the course three times and take four training runs, three of which will be officially timed.

During the actual running of the race, athletes start at intervals of 60 seconds. If a racer is obstructed in any way, he may appeal to a Jury member and request a re-run. If he makes it to the bottom without falling or missing any gates, the racer is asked to go to doping and suit control before being listed in the official results.

How World Skiers are Ranked

The world ranking of racers is done by a complicated system of classification called FIS penalty points. These are calculated for all competitors in all FIS-sanctioned races. Because it is a penalty system, the top-ranked racer is the one with the fewest points.

FIS penalty points are calculated by adding race points and race penalty. The winner of an FIS race receives 0.00 or a negative number of race points. The FIS provides tables at each event, which are used to determine race points for the rest of the competitors.

Race penalty takes into account the relative accomplishment of the competitive field. To calculate race penalty, the five competitors in the top ten finishers with the best current FIS standings are used. The sum of the best five FIS points on the current standings list is taken and multiplied by 2. The sum of these five skiers' race points (from the FIS tables provided at the event) is then subtracted from the total of current FIS points. This figure is then divided by 10 to give race penalty.

CALCULATION OF RACE PENALTY WORLD CUP GRODEN VAL GARDENA 1978

Rank	Name	Nation	FIS pts. on Current List	5 best pts. on Current List	Race pts. from FIS Tables
1	Haker, Erik	NOR	1.27	1.27	0.00
2	Mueller, Peter	SUI	3.13		
3	Read, Ken	CAN	2.01	2.01	10.28
4	Wirnsberger, Peter	AUT	2.61	2.61	10.42
5	Klammer, Franz	AUT	0.82	0.82	12.43
6	Antonioli, Renato	ITA	3.84		
7	Spiess, Ulrich	AUT	1.91	1.91	13.02
8	Murray, Dave	CAN	4.25		
9	Giardini, Guiliano	ITA	—		
10	Vesti, Walter	SUI	3.30		
				8.62	46.15

Sample Calculation:

Total 5 best FIS pts. 8.62 × 2 =	17.24
Minus total race points for 5 best	−46.15
	−28.91

$$-28.91 \div 10 = -2.89$$

The race penalty at Val Gardena was −2.89. In this event Ken Read would receive FIS penalty points totalling

$$10.28 + (-2.89) = 7.39$$

This figure would be averaged with points from previous races to determine rank and seeding for subsequent races. Until 1979 the best two results from the season were averaged and entered into the FIS book to determine overall points in world ranking. Under the new regulations the top three results are used. At the end of the season these results are used to determine seeding (starting position) for the following season.

The controls which have been placed upon the downhill by the FIS have made the sport a highly organized and regulated event. The enormous task of putting on a race and regulating the competitors is a difficult but necessary one, in order to maintain the high standards of world-wide competition.

CHAPTER SEVEN

Famous Downhills

For more than half a century alpine resorts around the world have groomed and transformed their mountainsides in an attempt to provide the ultimate challenge to the world's greatest ski racers. The challenge of creating world class courses on rough and varied mountain terrain has been tackled with zeal: the thousands of dollars and hours invested are testimony to the prestige attached to the hosting of a World Cup event.

Each approved World Cup course is unique and offers new adventures to the enthusiast following the White Circus and the ski racer. The seven courses described here include the world's oldest, its longest, its most famous and challenging, and one of its newest.

LAKE PLACID

Whiteface Mountain, site of the 1980 Men's and Women's Olympic downhill, is located about twelve miles from the small town of Lake Placid, N.Y. in the Adirondack Mountains. The surrounding area has excellent cross-country ski trails, ski jumps, ice-skating rinks, bobsled and luge runs and all the other facilities necessary at a location hosting a Winter Olympics.

Based on the standard of the world's classic downhills at Kitzbühel and Schladming in Austria or Wengen in Switzerland, the men's downhill at Whiteface will be a fair test: fast, but not particularly difficult and relatively short, at only 3028 meters. The average speed down the course will be 90 km/h (66 mph), giving finishing times of about 1:42 minutes.

In preparation for the 1980 Olympics an enormous snow-making plant was installed at Whiteface Mountain. Man-made snow skis very differently from natural snow and requires some adaptation by the skier in both technique and choice of skis and waxes. It is generally composed of more ice crystals and less air, making it very dense, somewhat like "old snow" — natural snow which has been skied on for several days. Natural packed powder is much more forgiving to small technical errors than man-made snow, which tends to ski more like ice because of its compact ice crystal content. Edges tend to catch and skis run straight out of turns. The Europeans, much less used to these special conditions, are apprehensive about the machine-made snow that will cover most of the courses at Whiteface. Most of the national teams have followed the lead of the Americans and experimented with ski bases and waxes in preparation for the 1980 Olympics.

Winter in Lake Placid, New York.

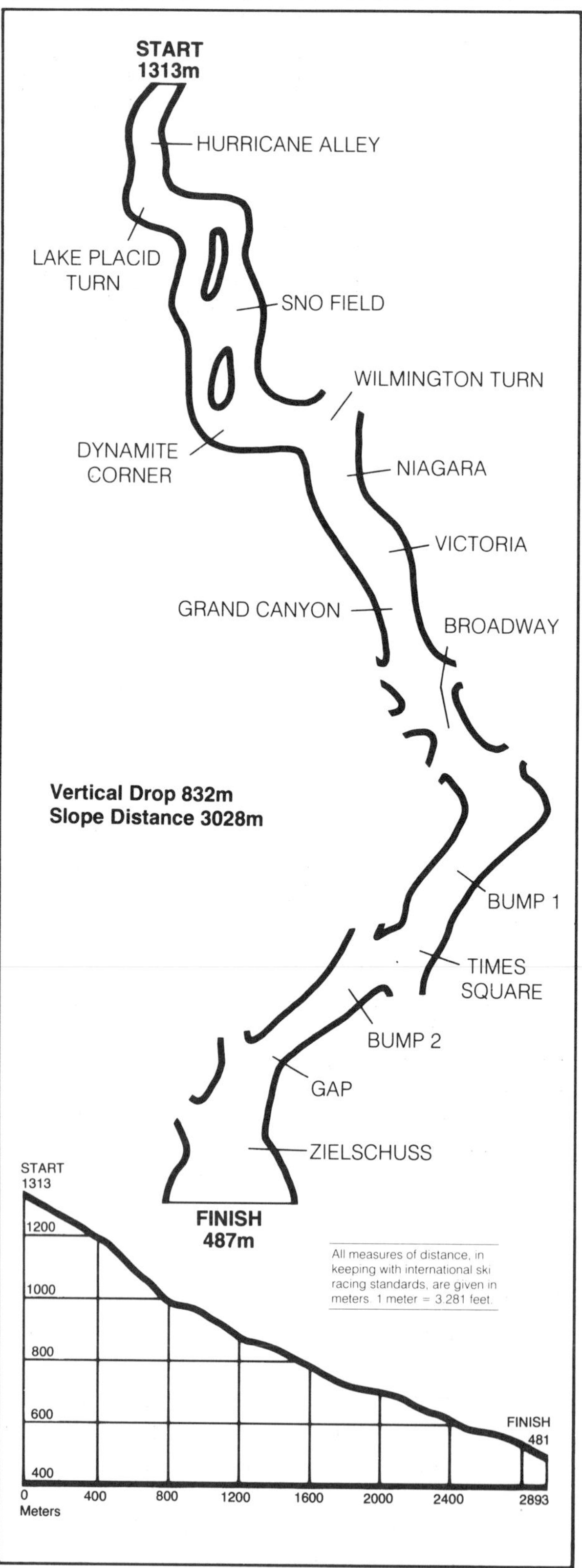

The men's downhill begins on **Hurricane Alley,** so called because of its exposure to high winds whipping across the start. The first few hundred meters of the course are not very steep, so the racer must make a particularly forceful push out of the starting gate to get him on his way down the mountain. The first 100 meters run straight down the fall line. The next 100 meters start a gradual turn to the left, during which the fall line crosses the trail and drops off very steeply into the **Lake Placid Turn.** The trail immediately becomes steeper again and veers more sharply to the left to the top of the **Sno Field.** Here the trail widens substantially and the course is laid out in an S-turn. This section, too, is quite steep, and because it must be watered to help snow stick to its face is consequently even icier than normal man-made snow.

The fall line crosses back again from right to left down to **Dynamite Corner**, where the course narrows and the racer must execute a sharp, fast left turn off the steep pitch preceding it. He must concentrate on staying low through the turn, where the terrain is fast and rough, making it hard to maintain good position. The course leads next into the **Wilmington Turn**, a sharp right running straight down the fall line and terminating at the top of **Niagara**, at which point the racer has finished the first quarter of the race.

Up to Dynamite Corner, the racer is cranking out the turns: there is little tucking involved,

Whiteface Mountain, Lake Placid

by permission of F.M.H.

The pre-Olympic victory ceremony: Peter Müller of Switzerland (second), Peter Wirnsberger of Austria (first), and David Murray of Canada (third).

Lindley photo

Ken Read trains on Dynamite Corner. The ABC network camera mount is one of 17 which covered the race from top to bottom at the pre-Olympic trials in 1979.

Dean Colour

Ken Read starts the final schuss of the Lake Placid Olympic course.

because he has his hands full just getting around the turns, but each one must be executed with speed and precision.

The long straightaway of Niagara is the steepest pitch on the Lake Placid course. At its base, the course turns off slightly to the left and the racer must stay in his tuck through this turn over the flats which lead into **Victoria.** This is the fastest section of the course: long, straight down the fall line and steep enough to build up to speeds of 130 km/h (80 mph) and more. At the bottom of Victoria is a small, but at those speeds tricky, bump which the racer normally rides. The **Grand Canyon** which follows is less steep and runs in a straight line toward **Broadway**. This is the half-way point on the race course.

Broadway is the flattest section of the men's downhill. The trail turns left over a series of insignificant bumps, then right under Lift #1. For the rest of the course, which is almost straight, the racer concentrates on riding a flat ski and staying in a good tuck. The slight right turn continues down the hill to **Bump 1**, where the racer must pre-jump a sort of bench or step in the terrain. The landing is tricky because it comes on a relatively flat part of the course and causes quite a jolt to the racer. The trail continues down the fall line of the mountain to **Times Square**, where it runs into the women's downhill course for a short distance, before diverging once again. Here, the racer has skied three-quarters of the course.

The trail through Times Square turns to the right under Lift #1 again and ends at **Bump 2**, which the racer can usually ride. Here the incline increases for a short distance before levelling off slightly into the **Gap**. The trail becomes steeper and turns gently to the left to the top of the **Zielschuss**. The racer maintains his tuck as the course steepens, turns slightly to the right and sucks two bumps just as the finish comes into sight.

The Whiteface downhill course has few bumps, rolls or sharp terrain changes, which means little air time for racers and close finish times. Good sliders — racers who can carry their speed across the flats — definitely have the advantage on this course.

The winner of the pre-Olympic downhill has often been among the Olympic medal winners the following year, so every eye is on Peter Wirnsberger of Austria, Peter Müller of Switzerland and David Murray of Canada, who placed first, second and third at Lake Placid in March, 1979.

The Austrians still have the favorites: Franz Klammer, Sepp Walcher, Werner Grissmann and Uli Spiess. Italian Herbert Plank won two World Cup downhills in 1978-79 and is very good on hard snow and fast turns, such as those at Whiteface. Other favorites are Michael Veith and Sepp Ferstl of Germany, Ken Read of Canada and Erik Haker from Norway. Americans Andy Mill and Karl Anderson should also make a good showing.

KITZBÜHEL

Kitzbühel, the Queen of the Northern Tyrol, is an old walled town dating back to the thirteenth century. People have been skiing here since 1892. It is one of the most famous mountain resorts in Europe, both summer and winter, and still the biggest ski center in Austria.

West of Kitzbühel a cablecar rises to the **Hahnenkamm**, site of the World Cup downhill. For many, this course tops the list of great downhills: Jean-Claude Killy calls it the perfect downhill. "It has every kind of problem a skier might encounter, thus demanding the utmost technical proficiency. There are very steep sections, rapid terrain changes, narrow sections, bumpy sections, changes in lighting, flats, jumps — the works. It's the kind of a race that could never be won on a fluke by some relative unknown. A list of the winners of the Hahnenkamm, in fact, is like a roll call of the world's skiing greats".

The World Cup downhill race is held annually on the **Streif.** This classic course begins at an altitude of 1660 meters (5478 feet) and drops for 860 meters (2838 feet) over 3.5 kilometers (1.9 miles). Because of this long vertical drop and the course's very steep and fast sections, the Hahnenkamm is regarded as the world's toughest downhill. It is always icy, because it is watered and fired with propane torches during preparation.

A slalom competition is held in conjunction with the downhill on a run called the Ganslernhang. The Hahnenkamm Cup is awarded to the racer with the best times in each of these disciplines. This combined event attracts jet-setters from around the world and it is not unusual to spy a Shah or a princess among the twenty or thirty thousand spectators.

The Hahnenkamm downhill course begins dramatically with two quick, icy turns, first right, then left, taking the skier right into the fall line and leading to a steep ledge or headwall known as the **Mausfalle** (mousetrap). On the approach to this big jump the racer must negotiate the sharp left turn and immediately pre-jump the ledge. He must stay as close as possible to the gate in order to be

▷▷*The top of the Mausfalle, which must be groomed smooth during race preparation.*

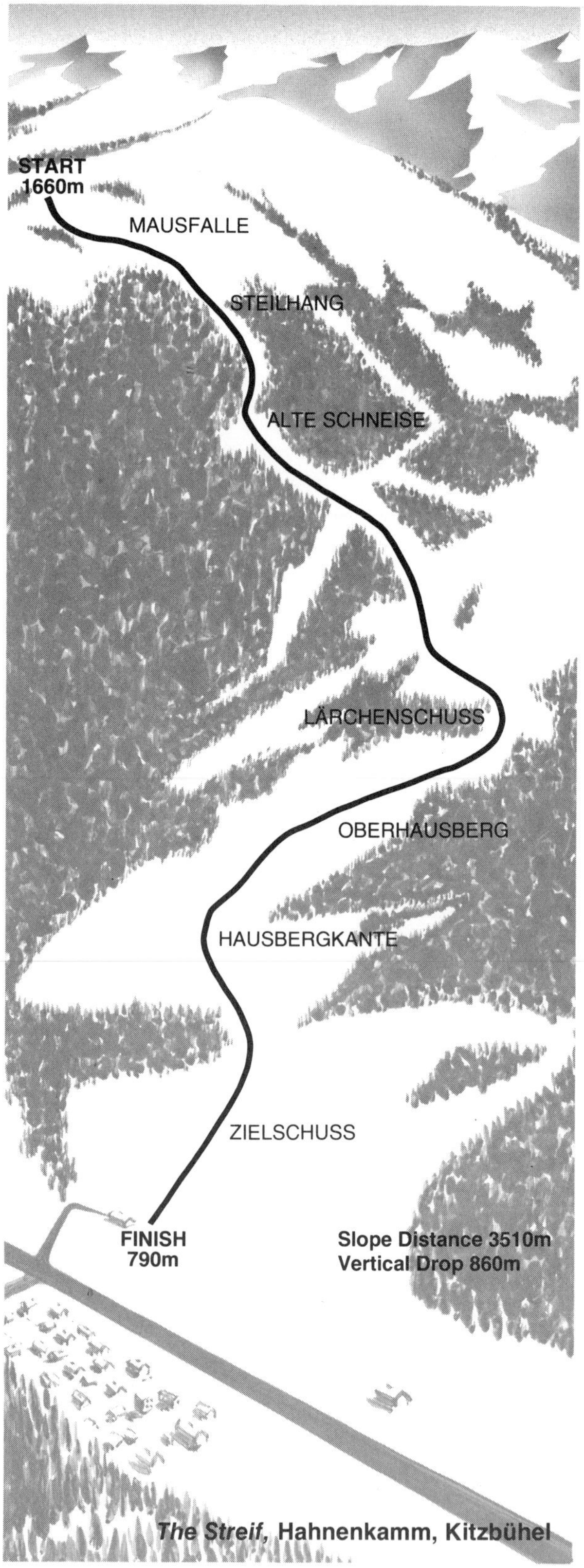

START
1660m
MAUSFALLE
STEILHANG
ALTE SCHNEISE
LÄRCHENSCHUSS
OBERHAUSBERG
HAUSBERGKANTE
ZIELSCHUSS
FINISH
790m
Slope Distance 3510m
Vertical Drop 860m

***The Streif*, Hahnenkamm, Kitzbühel**

courtesy of Kitzbühel

Lindley photo

A racer hangs on after getting air time off the Hausbergkante, an extremely difficult jump.

Franz Maier

Spectators on the roof of the small house which gives the Hausberg its name.

high enough to pre-jump the ledge properly: a mistake can send a skier flying 40 meters downhill, and even after a proper pre-jump a racer can be airborne for 25 or 30 meters. After landing on a long steep schuss, the course flattens quickly, creating a severe compression and the sudden deceleration puts tremendous pressure and strain on the racer's thigh muscles: the G-forces which he experiences are crushing. This compression is complicated by the fact that the racer must negotiate a sharp left corner at the bottom of the pitch.

An abrupt right turn precedes the next and most difficult section of the course: **the Steilhang** (steep wall). This section is so steep that snow will not cling to it and must be trucked in and stuck to the rock wall with water, which is then allowed to freeze. The right turn across this section is one of the most difficult on any ski racing course: a fallaway turn over very rough terrain. If a racer fails to negotiate it neatly, a fall could send him sliding at 120 km/h into a fence known as the **Bamboo Curtain**. This fence is an enormous construction of intertwined saplings, snow fences and hay bales, which protect the racer from the trees beyond.

The technical difficulty of the Steilhang is magnified by a cat-walk known as the **Alte Schneise**, a long, narrow, flat and tree-lined trail, which follows it. Only perfect execution through the Steilhang will allow the skier to maintain his speed through the Alte Schneise, a ride of approximately 45 seconds at top speed. This section ends in a side-hill pitch, which is almost always bumpy and rough from being sideslipped so frequently by recreational skiers. These bumps down the pitch and around the slight right turn at its bottom make riding a flat ski very difficult. At this point, the racer is just over halfway down the Hahnenkamm.

The course now opens up into a flat meadow which snakes right and left as it follows the natural terrain of the mountainside. A hard left turn and a sharp right mark the beginning of the **Hausberg**, so called because of the small house situated at the edge of the course. Its rooftop makes a particularly good vantage point for photographers and spectators to view the next challenge along the course, known as the **Hausbergkante**. The racer must set up his right turn perfectly because immediately after the abrupt drop off at the Hausbergkante there is a sharp left turn — the

Foto Tirol

The upper section of the Streif on Kitzbühel's Hahnenkamm.

Hausberg turn — onto a compression. It was at this spot in 1976 where Steve Podborski suffered a serious fall during a training run when he failed to set up his turn properly at the top of the ledge.

The course now opens up again into another open field along a steep side-hill, which is the fastest and toughest section of the course. The racer comes into full view of the spectators at the finish area as he makes a hard right turn and flies off the lip at the top of the Zielschuss.

Part way down the pitch there is a short flat section, immediately followed by a knoll, where the racer is momentarily out of view of the finish line. Here there is a dramatic pause, where spectators are never sure if a skier has successfully negotiated the bump or not.

This challenging run, a superb test of the downhiller's skill, has been modified for intermediate skiers, with the most difficult and dangerous sections by-passed by more moderate slopes. In good snow conditions, advanced skiers can enjoy its exciting sweep and rhythm, but even at slow speeds they might have difficulty getting down.

Foto Tirol

The town of Kitzbühel, Austria, seen from the Hahnenkamm, with Kitzbühel Horn in the background.

by permission of Salomon

Ken Read becomes light through a transition at the 1978 Schladming World Cup downhill, in which he placed first.

SCHLADMING

Since 1910 the Austrian town of Schladming has hosted national and international skiing competitions. A well-known winter sports center with swimming pools, training hills, skating rinks and cross-country ski trails, the area also played host to men's World Cup downhill events in 1973, 1975 and again in 1978 and is a candidate to host the 1982 World Alpine Ski Championships. The Canadian men's downhill team has traditionally done well at Schladming, with a first place win by David Irwin in 1975 and first and second placings in 1978 by Ken Read and David Murray respectively.

The course down the **Planai** is noted for its high speeds and tricky road jumps. It begins at an elevation of 1755 meters and finishes at 758 meters, a vertical drop of 997 meters, making it among the steepest of men's downhills. The 3.6 km course is set with 25-30 control gates. The terrain along the course is hilly but open, averaging 60 meters in width and protected from strong winds by thick forest on both sides of the track.

The Schladming downhill course is not particularly demanding technically. It begins on a long, steep, open pitch, and follows the terrain of the mountainside down to the classic **Zielschuss**, which is very long and steep, with a bump just before the finish.

However the course crosses over an access road to the top of the mountain at numerous points along the way, and these road jumps present a severe mental barrier to some racers.

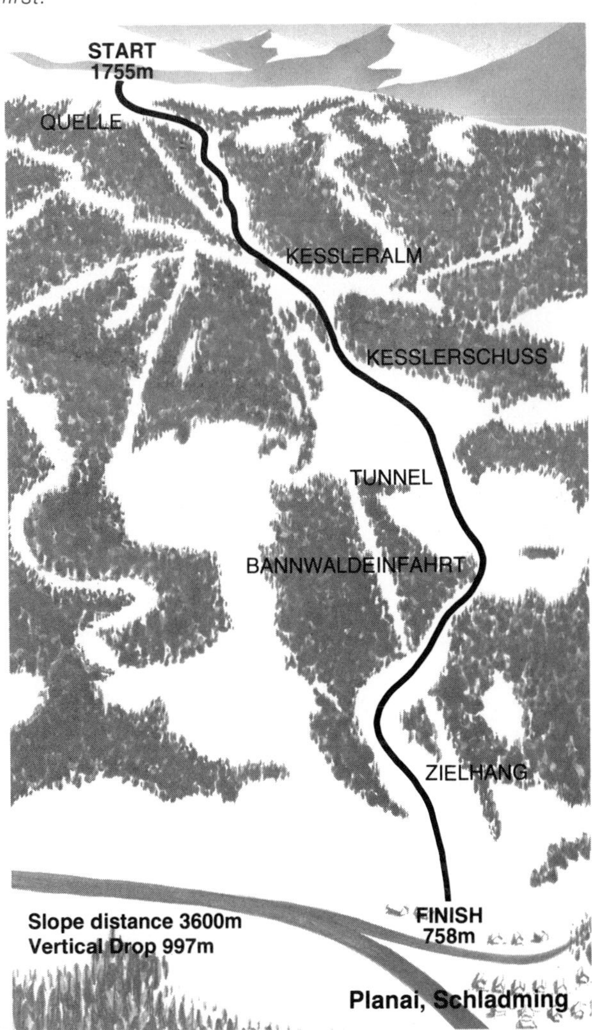

Foto Elfi

Zielschuss at Schladming 1978 showing adverse snow conditions. Snow had to be trucked in from the surrounding area by the army before the World Cup downhill could be run.

WENGEN

Wengen is a large mountain resort located near Bern in Switzerland. Accessible only by rail, this charming village has become famous for the Lauberhorn World Cup race, where every year the elite of the world's skiers meet again. Ski racing, a winter attraction in this British enclave for almost fifty years, was first conceived by the Englishman Sir Arnold Lunn, a resident at Wengen and organizer of the first ski competition ever held.

Racers gain access to the start of the **Hundschopf** run down the Lauberhorn by railway. The oldest and longest course in World Cup competition, it runs 4.26 km, with a vertical drop of 1028 meters. Franz Klammer still holds the course record, set in 1975, of 2:35:19.

This course has been labelled a "traditional" downhill, like Kitzbühel's Hahnenkamm, and does not meet all current FIS rulings concerning minimum course widths and distances. It is a unique course on many accounts.

The start is over a long, very fast meadow with a series of rolls. After a hard right and left turn the course moves into the 'cat's nuts', a narrow schuss between two rock bluffs, which ends at the **Minschkante.** This is a steep drop ending in a compression, at which point the racer must negotiate a tight 160° fallaway turn to the right. The trail then narrows and follows the railroad tracks. An S turn, first to the right and then to the left over a small bridge across a creek, drops suddenly and slows the racer in preparation for the tunnel, actually a railway underpass.

The course now moves onto a wide, tree-lined section of meadow, where there is a series of wide, sweeping turns over a bridge, under which recreational skiers can cross the course. The bridge marks the start of the **Hanneggschuss,** a narrow, steep schuss, at the beginning of which the skier comes very close to the trees on the right side of the course. The trail then flattens into the **Österreicher Loch** or Austrian hole, a severe compression in a flat containing three big rolls, where several members of the Austrian team have fallen in recent years. The Hole ends in a last section of S-turns — real leg-burners, demanding great stamina. The whole section is watered making it icy and very fast: the entire S turn is completed in 5 to 6 seconds. Each

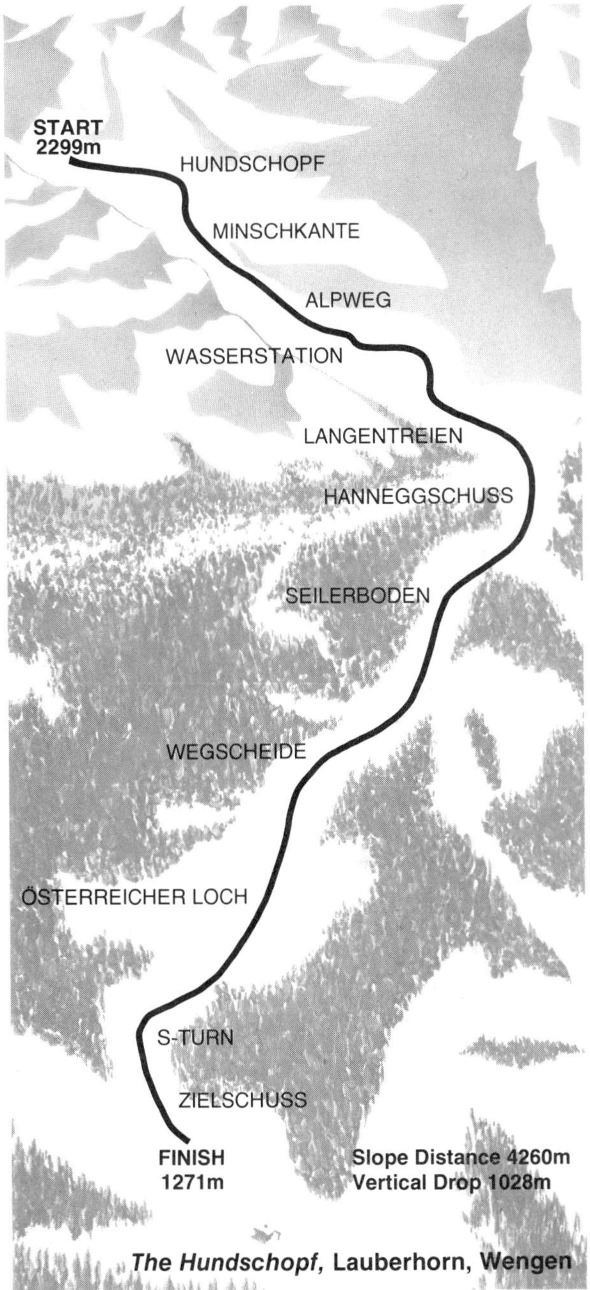

The Hundschopf, **Lauberhorn, Wengen**

turn in the S — left-right-left — is banked or tilted in the wrong direction, so the ski must be turned "off camber" — very light weight distribution over it. The first corner is blind and the second turn must be made in a compression, as the course flattens abruptly and the skier is thrown into the third turn immediately. Half-way through the last 'left-hander' the terrain drops off suddenly for the final dash to the finish over the **Zielschuss**.

courtesy of Wengen

Aerial view of the Hundschopf at Wengen.

courtesy of Wengen

Start area of the Lauberhorn downhill.

courtesy of Wengen

Downhill finish area of the Lauberhorn.

An aerial photograph of "la descente" on the Piste des Haut-Forts at Morzine.

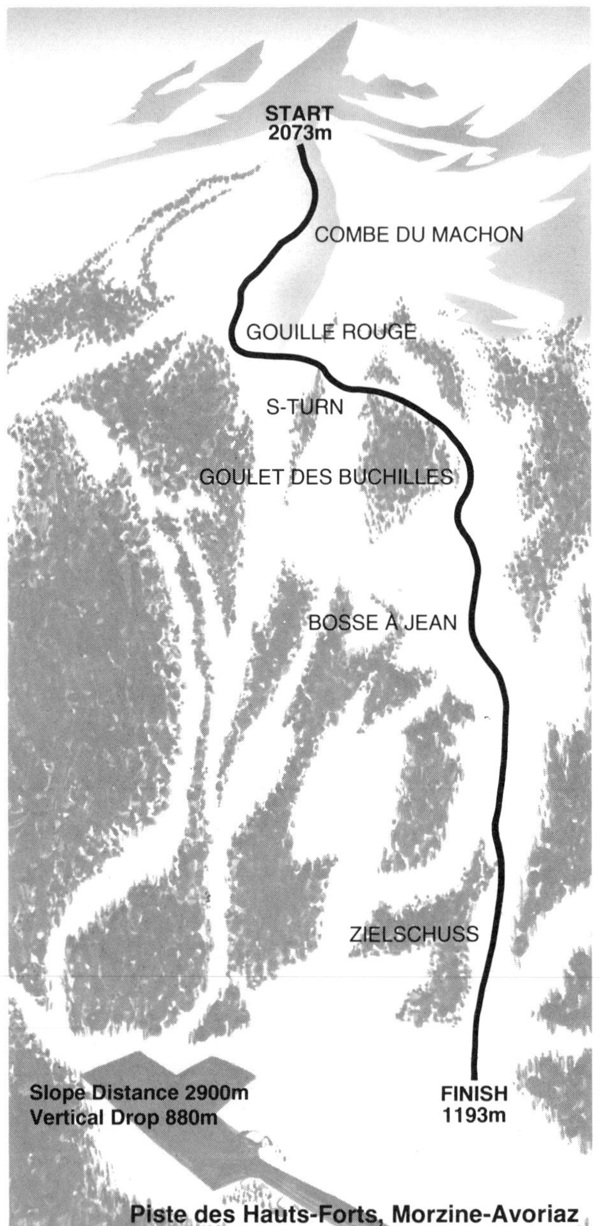

Piste des Hauts-Forts, Morzine-Avoriaz

MORZINE-AVORIAZ

Morzine-Avoriaz, located on the Franco-Swiss border, has grown in the past twenty years from a small traditional resort offering the bare minimum to holiday skiers, into a vigorous ski 'circus', organizing high level ski competitions.

The men's downhill course on the **Piste des Hauts-Forts** is considered one of the most technically demanding in the world, with its long side-hill traverses, varied snow conditions from top to bottom and high speed turns. The course is located on the great Intrêt ridge and begins at an elevation of 2073 meters (6500 feet). Over its 2.9 km length it drops 880 vertical meters in an approximate time of 1:43 (course record). After the start the racer descends **La Combe du Machon**, a long, steep traverse 205 meters (615 feet) long. The course then turns sharply and the racer enters the **Carousel**, a long, sweeping S-turn. It is important to execute this section as perfectly as possible to maintain speed through the **Gouille rouge**. Although the track continues through the gorge and the incline becomes less steep, the skier can gain speed here because there are no turns.

The course follows the natural curve of the landscape through a long gentle turn to the lower part of the Intrêt ridge, where the racer encounters the **S-turn,** one of the most spectacular sections of the course. The S begins with an abrupt right turn followed by a left, which has to be made on a hill ending in a traverse. Next comes a schuss through a narrow gully, which flattens out suddenly into a compression, where the the racer must make a fast right turn.

This rather difficult turn leads to a bump, over which the racer must pre-jump, followed by a slight traverse across the fall line into three consecutive turns (left-right-left). The racer finally arrives at the **Zielschuss** which crosses the **Gotte Rose** bridge and gradually flattens out to the finish.

courtesy of Morzine

Morzine — Avoriaz in winter.

VAL D'ISÈRE

The spectacular World Cup downhill in Val d'Isère, France is normally held in early December, one of the first major races on the circuit. It presents a fresh challenge for the racer and is a good indicator of the new racing year for the spectator.

The **Piste Oreiller-Killy** was designed by Jean-Claude Killy, after whom it was named, and the local ski club president, M. Louis Erny and was constructed in 1967, the same year in which Killy and Nancy Greene became the first winners of the World Cup championship.

Although the Piste O-K, as it is called, demands the highest technical proficiency from racers, it is not a dangerous course. The trail is wide with no sharp bumps and the chances of hitting the trees in a fall are minimal, except at the Compression. It is, however, long enough to test the racer's endurance, varied enough in terrain to present challenges and steep enough to demand courage.

The flatter sections of the course place demands upon the ski technicians and coaches to choose the proper wax and skis and on the racers to keep a flat ski and a perfect aerodynamic position. The course is a spectators' dream, designed so that they can ski down either side of the piste while the race is in progress.

The racer gets up good speed right at the **Startschuss**, which is followed by a long flat where good waxing and tuck position are both important. A very steep headwall follows the flats. Here, the racer must choose an inside line in order to prepare for a long pre-jump over **Collumbin's Bump**. This pre-jump, even when taken properly, hurls the racer 20 to 25 meters to a landing on a step schuss below.

Where the course reaches the timberline, trees suddenly shade the trail and the transition from bright sunlight is an abrupt shock to a racer travelling at maximum speed. The course quickly flattens into a compression, followed immediately by a flat. From this flat section the first turn of the 'S' is a sharp corner to the left on a small hill. At this point the racer finds himself totally unweighted and the turn must be negotiated almost in mid-air. The outrun of the S-turn leads the racer into a traverse which is long but not very steep. It is important to keep a tight inside line throughout the

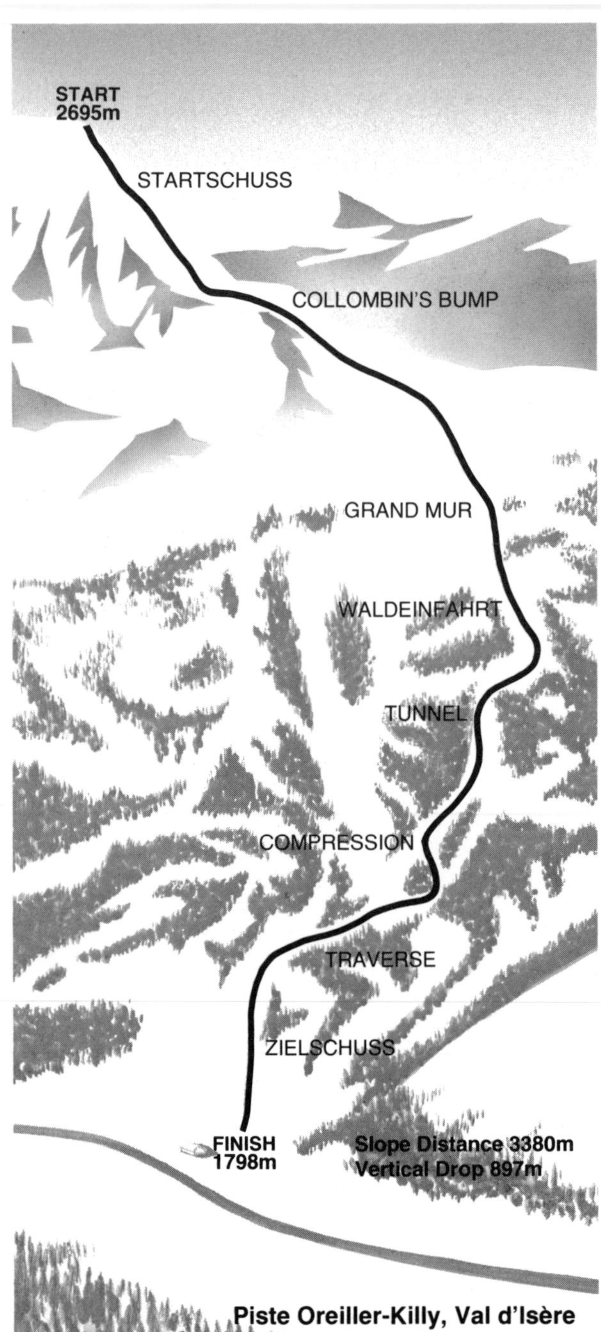

Piste Oreiller-Killy, Val d'Isère

S-turn to maintain speed on the outrun. Otherwise the competitor will lose speed on this section, which leads to a compression turn. After the compression turn, a left turn begins through an uphill section which throws the racer into the air. He must negotiate a right turn upon landing, then a sweeping left turn to the finish over the tree-lined **Zielschuss.**

Air time off a big roller at the top of the Fallaway at Lake Louise.

by permission of Shell Canada Ltd.

LAKE LOUISE

The Lake Louise ski region is located in the Canadian Rockies approximately 56 km northwest of Banff, Alberta. The downhill course on Mount Whitehorn has been rated an Olympic calibre downhill by FIS and although a World Cup event has yet to be held here, its class rivals that of Schladming in Austria. The course is fast, with average speeds of 110 km/h and a maximum incline of 42° (90%). If offers all the challenges of a great downhill: fallaway turns and bumps, technical S-turns, compressions and combination bumps leading to compressions. It is one of Canada's two top class downhill courses, offering the best for world class competition.

The course laid out along Mt. Whitehorn's south-east face is protected from prevailing weather and very well lit. Starting at an elevation of 2505 meters, the men's downhill has a vertical drop of 842 meters to a finishing elevation of 1663 meters. It is long and demanding (3.2 km), with steep pitches and tight corners. The start, located well above the timberline, is very quick and steep. After a vertical drop of 240 meters (800 feet) the course takes a sharp left corner on to a long traversing section known as **Wiwaxy**. Through this section racers must pay special attention to keeping a low compact body position and riding a flat ski, to gain speed as they approach the S-turns or **Pitch** — a section of five linked turns through rolling, tree-lined terrain. They begin with a very hard right turn complicated by two double bumps, which immediately fall away down one of the steepest sections of the course. At this point the skier has completed the first third of the race.

Towards the bottom of the S-turns there is a slight compression at which racers must choose a high line to be in proper position to approach the **Fallaway**, a diagonal traverse over the steepest section of the course. Since the terrain is smooth and hard the racer picks up speed as he makes a long, sweeping right turn very close to the trees, from which he is separated by safety netting. At the bottom of the Fallaway there is a severe compression as the racer enters the **Cannon Barrels**, a narrow tree-lined section at which the track flattens. The light here changes from bright sunlight to deep shade. The Cannon Barrels shoot the racer into **Double Trouble**, a section of twin

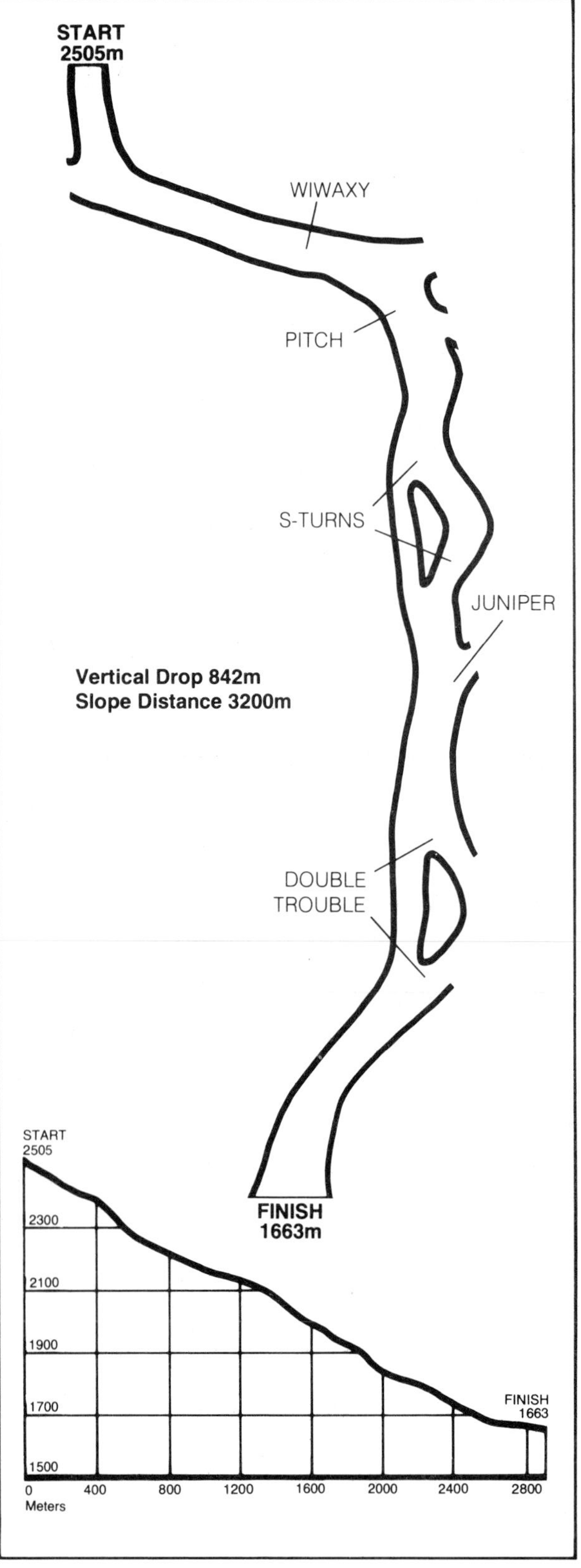

START
FINISH
Mount Whitehorn, Lake Louise

courtesy of Lake Louise

The Canadian Rockies from Lake Louise ski area.

bumps. The first pre-jump lands the skier in a compression, after which he must immediately make a second pre-jump.

If the racer fails to absorb these bumps by pre-jumping, he faces serious injury in the woods which line the course at this point. The severe compression in this section demands every shred of stamina the racer can muster.

As at Kitzbühel, the final schuss down Mt. Whitehorn comes as a welcome relief. The trail widens and the slope becomes quite smooth and flat, veering slightly to the right before descending a short hill to the finish line.

Lake Louise has played host to the Shell Cup Canadian Championships on many occasions and racers from other nations often compete here both for practice on the North American piste and to upgrade their FIS points.

courtesy of Lake Louise

The south-east face of Mt. Whitehorn, site of the Lake Louise downhill.

Franz Maier

Glossary

Abductors One of the major muscle groups used in skiing, which move the limbs away from the axis of the body (opposite of adductors).

Acceleration The technique used by the skier to move out of a carved turn at a greater speed than that at which he entered it.

Adductors The muscles used in skiing, which draw the limbs toward the axis of the body (opposite of abductors).

Aerobic (as used in ski terminology) The ability of the muscles of the body to utilize oxygen while producing an effort. As this ability increases, so does a skier's endurance.

Aerodynamics The branch of dynamics which deals with the motion of air and with the forces acting on bodies in motion in the air. The most aerodynamic position on skis is the tuck or crouch.

Agility The ability of an individual to move quickly and easily.

Alpine Skiing Events Timed downhill, giant slalom and slalom competitions.

Anticipation In skiing, the act of looking far enough ahead that the skier is prepared for upcoming changes in terrain.

Base The running surface of the ski, which has a groove running down its center to allow the ski to run fast and track straight. On racing skis, it is composed of plastic compounds which have been specially developed to match various snow conditions.

Calcification (Myositis ossificans) Deposits of calcium and magnesium insoluble salts in a body tissue, often occurring during the healing process of a severely damaged bone.

Calisthenics Systematic, rhythmic body exercises, usually performed without apparatus, that build strength and endurance.

Camber The slight arch or upward curve along the base of the ski.

Cardiovascular System Circulation of the blood through the heart and blood vessels, which provides the body with oxygen to burn as fuel.

Carved Turn A turn made on the edges of the ski with the least possible sideslip.

Centrifugal Force The force which propels the skier away from the center of a turn.

Circuit A series of races in different locations.

Circuit Training A regimen of exercises done in sequence without resting in between, which builds strength and endurance.

Combined Event An event in ski competition in which a skier's results in two separate disciplines (e.g. downhill and slalom) are combined to determine the best overall skier at the event.

Complete Turn A turn which describes a complete arc.

Compression A sudden change in terrain where it becomes very flat.

Concussion The jarring of the brain due to a blow or fall.

Control Gates A series of poles which outline the direction of the course and through which the racer must pass to complete the course properly.

Criterium de la première neige The first important race of the season.

Crouch A low, stable aerodynamic position used by ski racers to attain maximum speed (See also TUCK).

Downhill Ski The ski which is on the bottom or outside arc of the turn.

Edge The metal sides of a ski which hold it steady through a turn by acting as a blade cutting through the snow.

Edging The practice of holding the skis on their edges during a carved turn.

Edge Control Holding the edge to prevent chattering of the ski.

Endurance The ability of an athlete to sustain maximum effort over a long period of time, using the cardiovascular system to deliver oxygen to all working body tissues.

Europa Cup Circuit A series of alpine FIS-sanctioned races in Europe. The level of competition is one step below World Cup level.

Fall Line The gravitational line of a hill.

FIS International Ski Federation. An international organization governing ski competition and representing and governing all amateur skiers. It is comprised of all National Ski Associations.

Flats The long sections of a downhill course which, though not flat, are less steep than the pitches.

Flex The bending capability of a ski.

Force Majeure Any special set of circumstances which necessitates a change in FIS regulations.

Forerunner A skier with non-competitive status who skis the course before each training run or race to test timing equipment and communication systems, and prepare the snow surface for top-seeded racers.

Forward Position A slight forward lean of the body through the ankles, caused by the construction of the ski boot.

Giant Slalom (GS) The alpine event in which a skier executes more open and rhythmic turns than are called for in the slalom event.

Glide A technique primarily used on the flats during a race, in which the skis are kept perfectly flat against the snow.

Hamstrings Any of the tendons which bind the muscles behind the thigh (the ham) to the hollow of the knee.

Homologation The documented ratification or approval of any course by the FIS.

Icing A condition of the snow caused by melting and refreezing on its upper surface.

Initiation The first phase of a turn, accomplished by the pole plant and unweighting.

Inside Edge The edge of the ski which is closest to the inside of the turn.

Inspection A pre-race procedure during which the competitors slowly sideslip the course to inspect and memorize its contours.

Interval Downhill Course A downhill course used during training, in which there are sections where the skier can rest.

Interval Training Any training which allows the athlete to rest after performing an exercise and prior to its repetition.

Isometrics Exercises in which opposing muscles are contracted so that there is little shortening but great increase in tone of muscles involved.

Lower Body In skiing this refers to the legs, knees, ankles and feet.

Long Rolling Track A section of course with smooth rolling terrain sometimes used in training downhill racers.

Major Muscle Groups The muscles of the upper legs and mid-section of the body which are used most in skiing.

Mobility The ability to move the joints with ease.

Molson World Cup One of the FIS sanctioned World Cup events held in Canada.

Nordic Events Cross-country skiing and ski jumping.

Oxygen Debt A condition in which the muscles must perform although there is a deficiency of oxygen supply to the blood stream (anerobic).

Oblique Descent A traverse across the fall line.

Piste The mountain slopes and trails upon which downhill is raced.

Pitch A steep section of the downhill course.

Pontiac Cup A Canadian FIS event for younger racers.

Pre-Jump A technique used by a racer to cross bumps at high speeds, during which he takes air just before reaching the lift of the bump and actually jumps over the bump.

Psyche An expression used by ski racers to designate mental and emotional preparation before a race.

Quadriceps The great muscle group at the front of the thigh above the knee.

Relaxed Attack A style of skiing in which the racer remains loose and yet aggressive.

Ruts Well-worn sections of the course.

S Turn A turn designated by three control gates which form a figure 'S' on a pitch.

Seeding Placement of racers into their starting groups. Racers with the best FIS standings are "top-seeded", while the weakest racers are "last-seeded".

Shell Cup A sponsored ski event held yearly in Canada.

Side Cut The difference in the width of the ski from tip to tail.

Sideslip The sideways sliding action of the skis.

Slalom The alpine discipline, in which a competitor executes many short radius turns around control gates.

Snow Resistance The friction caused by the running surface of a ski against the snow surface.

Speed In fitness training, speed is the ability to move the joints quickly.

Stamina The ability to perform in a physical state of oxygen debt (anerobic).

Straight Running A descent straight down the fall line of a slope.

Strength The ability of a muscle to overcome resistance.

Suck A technique used in downhill skiing to absorb bumps with the legs.

Timing Wand The part of the electronic timing equipment at the starting gates which must be opened by the racer to start the clocks running.

Traverse An oblique descent across a slope.

Tuck A low aerodynamic position used by ski racers (See also CROUCH).

Unweighting A slight upward body movement which temporarily lightens the body weight on the skis, used most often during a turn.

Uphill Ski The ski closest to the top of the slope.

White Circus The World Cup circuit.

Wind Sprints Running short distances at maximum speed to build stamina.

Wind Tunnel A large scientific testing apparatus to determine the aerodynamics of an object or body.

World Championships Held every two years to determine the top Alpine skiers.

World Cup Points Awarded to the top fifteen finishers in all four World Cup events to determine the overall winners of the World Cup.